150 POCKET THOUGHTS
RICHARD BEWES
LET THE BIBLE REINVIGORATE YOUR DAY

150 POCKET THOUGHTS
RICHARD BEWES
LET THE BIBLE REINVIGORATE YOUR DAY

CHRISTIAN FOCUS

Copyright © Richard Bewes 2004

ISBN 1-85792-991-8

Published in 2004
by
Christian Focus Publications,
Geanies House,
Fearn, Tain, Ross-shire,
IV20 1TW, Scotland, UK

www.christianfocus.com

Cover design by Alister MacInnes

Printed and bound by
Rotanor, Norway

INTRODUCTION

The telephone shrilled by my bedside. It seemed incredibly early. It was Christine Morgan of the BBC.

'Richard? I'm sorry to rouse you – but your "Thought for the Day" is going to have to be changed. The Gulf War is over!'

'Over? Oh my! I'll get cracking immediately.'

My producer and I had been getting the script finalised at 11.00 pm the night before. 'Thought for the Day' always went out live on BBC's Today programme, and – coming as it did somewhere between news summaries and the weather forecast – you were expected to be right up-to-the-minute, with relevant, animated chatter. Now, on the morning itself, everything had to be changed.

'You'll still be in your pyjamas,' went on Christine, 'but can you start right away on the script, while I find out more about the situation? Then I'll get back to you for a check on how you're doing. I'll give you forty minutes. You'll just have time then to get dressed. We'll send a taxi to bring you in to Broadcasting House!'

I've been delivering 'thoughts' for years. In more recent times many of them have been web-site contributions. The fact is that 'thoughts' are coming at us throughout the day, and all that is required is to develop an instinct for them. The Kikuyu people of Kenya have a special word for such thoughts. It is 'Meciria' ('Mesheeria'), creative thoughts, deep thoughts, powerful and penetrating – even life-transforming in their effect.

Sometimes I have received little warning, and have had to come up with what is virtually an *instant thought*. And yet – however sudden the call – such thoughts are never instant, not really. They come out of a regular drawing upon an inexhaustible reservoir – the Bible; the very thoughts of God himself.

How precious to me are your thoughts, O God! How vast is the sum of them! Were I to count them, they would outnumber the grains of sand. When I awake, I am still with you (Psalm 139:17).

Nothing that God has said is feeble. The Scriptures are teeming with stories, divine promises, vivid characters and sentences that glow with significance, if only we have an eye for them.

Understand these as *God's* thoughts, and – however short their duration – they will never be trite or trivial. God can arrest us with just a word! Ten minutes' thought may well be enough to comfort, challenge or change an individual for ever. It has happened so often.

I take a pocket Bible into every day with me – do you? In carrying the Scriptures on my person I know that I have a fathomless resource right at hand – and I can refer to it; on the underground train, in the lunch break or speaking with an individual. 'Thoughts' then begin to surface. Little incidents get attached to them. It is an art that we can develop – of making something out of apparently nothing!

Use these hundred and fifty 'thoughts' as you will. While they are not sermons, nevertheless there could be readers who wish to turn some of them into more developed messages; go right ahead. D.L. Moody of Chicago once gave this advice, 'If you have something that is good for anything at all, pass it around!'

Richard Bewes
All Souls Church
August 2004

1. Begin with Jesus

In the beginning was the Word, and the Word was with God, and the Word was God *(John 1:1).*

People sometimes complain, *I can't see where Jesus fits in.* A theologian called Athanasius, Egyptian by birth and Greek by education, gave the answer sixteen hundred years ago: 'The only system of thought into which Jesus Christ will fit is the one in which He is the starting point'.

If we've begun with our own human-based attempt at the understanding of life and its meaning, we will actually never get it right – let alone the place that Christ occupies. We will be like the man who tries to do up his shirt buttons, **beginning with the wrong button**. He may hope that it will end up all right in the end ... but it never will!

This is the great point of John chapter 1. *Begin with Jesus,* ('the Word', who brings about and executes God's saving plan from of old) and you'll get it right. The existence of Christ didn't start at Bethlehem! From eternity, His was the executive role in the three Persons of the only true and Trinitarian God. Without Him we could never have even seen God. But through Him, *God is brought within touching distance.* Read John chapter 1, and you'll see!

Through Him, *God is brought within touching distance.*

2. Leadership and service

So I went to the angel and asked him to give me the little scroll. He said to me, 'Take it and eat it. It will turn your stomach sour, but in your mouth it will be as sweet as honey' *(Revelation 10:9).*

Leadership and service are so important to Christians, they could almost be said to be our food. In a letter of 1757 William Grimshaw, the celebrated Vicar of Haworth in Yorkshire wrote, 'Preaching is health, food and physic to me'.

Here in Revelation 10, the call of the evangelist John is confirmed, with the giving to him of a 'little scroll'. This is his commission – and it is to become his food.

But John's work will taste bitter-sweet. Do you know this yourself, Christian? Is it not the sweetest, the most wonderful work of all, to be in service to the Master of the World? At the same time, does it not present us with a bitter tang, when we find ourselves on the receiving end of the anger that Christ's mission generates? It is all to do with the Cross.

Don't be surprised. If your work for Him is authentic, you will be aware of pain, running alongside the joy. When that happens, you will know yourself to be confirmed in the same calling that was John's!

To look up: John 4:34

> **If your work for Him is authentic, you will be aware of pain, running alongside the joy.**

3. The first miracle

You have kept the best wine until now! *(John 2:10).*

As a taker of weddings, I've seen it all. I've seen the front end of one wedding run into the back end of the previous one ... brides arriving 45 minutes late ... guests turning up at the very end ... mothers in tears, bridegrooms passing out; we once had the photographer crashing into the three-tier wedding cake.

But water into wine ... think of having, as one of your wedding guests, God in human form! This tells me something about Jesus:

Jesus takes hold of the ordinary
A wedding, eh? Nothing more everyday, more human than that. That is the wonder of God becoming human. It means He is interested in our human affairs. He is concerned with the ordinary.

The ordinary becomes better
'You have kept the good wine until now!' And that has always been the testimony of Christian experience; there is an extra added-value to life with Christ. Wherever He is at work, there is an elevation.

The best is yet to come
This first miracle of Jesus Christ – the turning of the water into wine – was great enough, but it was only the beginning! By now some 2 billion of us have become part of the story – on all five continents. And it isn't over yet.

**This first miracle of Jesus Christ was great enough,
but it was only the beginning!**

4. Enoch

By faith, Enoch was taken from this life, so that he did not experience death; he could not be found, because God had taken him away. For before he was taken, he was commended as one who walked with God *(Hebrews 11:5).*

Nothing is more important in the end than to walk with God; as one Bible translation puts it, 'He pleased God'.

Nothing much else is known about Enoch. His sayings? His achievements? His hobbies? It's a blank – except for the one vital epitaph. And he was one of only two men who never died, the other being Elijah. God took him to himself, direct.

One day Enoch simply failed to turn up for lunch. Methuselah his son must have said to the others, 'Where's Dad? I can't find him'. The news went round the village....*Enoch's missing.*

'He could not be found'. The implication is that there was a search party! Maybe they wouldn't have bothered to look too far for some of the characters who feature in the book of Genesis. But Enoch was different. He left a yawning gap in the community. He had walked with God, and so he was missed.

Anyone can walk with God. You may live in obscurity and never hit the headlines. But you'll be the key person around. And they'll miss you when you've gone.

He had walked with God, and so he was missed.

5. The secret of success

'Not by might, nor by power, but by my Spirit', says the Lord Almighty *(Zechariah 4:6).*

Here lies the secret of lasting success. God's words were given to the prophet Zechariah around 520 BC, after the national humiliation and exile of the Jewish people. It was a time of rebuilding of the Temple – and of the national life once more. Here are principles that stand for ever!

Ideas are sharper than swords
A few people, armed with a spiritual ideal, can do so much more than a well-equipped army. Gideon and his valiant 300 ... David and Goliath – it's the lesson of the few. It's not the military machines, nor the politicians who hold the vital key to the destiny of the world, but the ideas people.

Spirit is superior to flesh
So the danger moments for Christianity have been when the churches went down the road of material, or even military, advancement – and got fat. At such points we become unusable to God. It is noticeable that revivals don't usually occur in areas of prosperity.

Good is stronger than evil
Learn from Zechariah! What we see in the violence and sensuality of our own time are not the vibrant triumphs of a kingdom in ascendancy, but the thrashing death-throes of a kingdom in desperation – that is destined for defeat.

> **A few people, armed with a spiritual ideal, can do so much more than a well-equipped army.**

6. The power of prayer

Peter therefore was kept in prison; but prayer was made without ceasing of the church unto God for him *(Acts 12:5 KJV)*.

Yes, heads were getting cracked right and left. Stephen and James had both been eliminated; now it was Peter, the Rock Man who had got clapped into a top security wing under heavy guard. The story ends well, with the angelic intervention, the snapping of the prisoner's shackles, and the freeing of Peter – whereupon he heads straight for the church prayer gathering.

The covenant of prayer
Prayer was central to the church's life; there was an agreement about it – 'we are going to pray'. Herod Agrippa thought he had disposed of the early church by incarcerating its leader, but prayer brings God into the arena!

The community of prayer
A tingling sense of expectancy characterises the church that prays. Church worship, fellowship and outreach become irradiated with the presence and power of Christ himself when prayer is recognised as the most important activity of all!

The combustion of prayer
When Peter gets to the prayer meeting, the members were 'amazed' ... a masterly understatement. Peter's arrival fairly lit up the prayer meeting that night! Typically, we are invariably surprised when God uses our feeble prayers to bring about His will.

The church that prays will always be in for suprises!

7. Meaningless?

Yet when I surveyed all that my hands had done and what I had toiled to achieve, everything was meaningless, a chasing after the wind *(Ecclesiastes 2:11).*

'Most people', commented Theophan the Recluse, 'are like a shaving of wood which is curled round its central emptiness'. The book of Ecclesiastes brilliantly exposes the emptiness of life without God.

In the opening sentences of chapter 2, the Teacher, as he is called, sees wealth in a number of different ways; in terms of the sensual (vv. 1-3), the cultural (vv. 4-7), the material (v. 8), and the powerful (vv. 9, 10).

We sense a change at verse 11: 'Yet, when I surveyed....' What causes an individual to think again about life and its significance? Very often, success itself is the trigger. 'Nothing fails like success', said Dean Inge of St Paul's Cathedral in London. We scale the summit of our ambitions and are left looking at an empty sky – *so what next?*

Solomon had expressed centuries ago, the experience that has come to so many – to gain power and adulation, to be adored by millions, to have financial security *and yet never be together as a person.*

Be grateful for those trigger points that help it come together; a Christian friend, a live church, a helpful book or a conference. Who wants life to be no more than a curled-up wood shaving?

**Who wants life to be no more
than a curled-up wood shaving?**

8. A strange history

Now when they heard of the resurrection of the dead, some mocked (Acts 17: 32).

It wasn't too surprising perhaps. After all, there in Athens, just behind the Christian apostle Paul, was the mighty temple of the Parthenon – looking as fresh and white as it was when first built 500 years earlier. Who was this idiot who had arrived in sophisticated Athens, with talk of a man who had died, only to be raised from death? Did Paul imagine he could overturn the towering world-view that prevailed right across Europe, and replace it with another?

But that's exactly what Paul did have in mind. His hearers wouldn't laugh for ever! The day would come when the Parthenon itself would be dedicated as a Christian church – and a church it remained for a thousand years, until the Turks took and held Athens for a period. It was a Venetian shell in 1687 that finally reduced the Parthenon to its present-day state.

A strange history! Christianity held the Parthenon longer even than the religion of the Greeks. Not that the control of a mere building is of any ultimate importance. More important is the durability of a thought-form. That is the message of the Parthenon. The story has held. Think on that, and on Paul the apostle, when you get the chance of a visit.

The story has held!

9. Check your Bible

Now the Bereans were of more noble character than the Thessalonians, for they received the message with great eagerness and examined the Scriptures every day to see if what Paul said was true *(Acts 17:11).*

You've heard of Diet Cokes? ...they're okay. But don't ever be content with a *Diet Bible*. Here's where the Bereans scored. They studied all the Scriptures, so that when even the mighty apostle Paul arrived, they checked up on him! *Is Paul bringing in an alternative Gospel? How far is he in line with the prophets of old?*

All was well. In fact as Paul himself later declared in Acts 26:22, 23: **I am saying nothing beyond what the prophets and Moses said would happen – that the Christ would suffer and, as the first to rise from the dead, would proclaim light to His own people and to the Gentiles**. 'No', Paul was saying, 'there's nothing original about me! I'm not saying anything that isn't already in the Scriptures'.

But they had checked already. Be a Berean! Carry the Bible with you into every day; always have one with you. If you haven't got the right size, save up for one, or put it on your birthday list. And every time you go to a Christian meeting or listen to a preacher, pull out that Bible and **check up**.

Carry the Bible with you into every day.

10. Freedom of the city

**For all things are yours, whether Paul or Apollos or Cephas or the
world or life or death or the present or the future, all are yours; and
you are Christ's; and Christ is God's** *(1 Corinthians 3: 21-23).*

Once on a preaching visit to Charlotte in North Carolina, I
was amazed to be given the freedom of the city. The airport, the
skyscrapers and multi-level expressways – 'It's yours!' they said.

Here in this Bible passage, the apostle Paul was writing to the
harassed Christians of Corinth, '**All things are yours**', he declared.
Paul was referring to something wider than the theatre, swimming
baths, basilica and stadium. This was the freedom not of a single
city but of the Universe ... of Time, Eternity and the Future. They
had it all in Christ. **All are yours; and you are Christ's; and Christ
is God's.**

We need the last phrase to tie up the argument. Jesus wasn't
yet one more leader of some faction or belief-system. *He is part
of the very Godhead.* 'If you have Him', runs the argument, ' you
have everything – including the shining and eternal City of God'.
Christians are the only people on earth who belong to two cities at
one and the same time.

**Christians are the only people on earth who belong to two cities at
one and the same time.**

11. Raise the standard

When the enemy shall come in like a flood, the Spirit of the Lord shall lift up a standard against him *(Isaiah 59:19 KJV).*

Yes, the King James Version is best at this point. So insists the modern Bible scholar Alec Motyer. The power of evil, says Isaiah, sometimes sweeps upon a society like a flood, but the people of faith can gather and fight – with spiritual weapons – united under a 'standard'.

What is this *standard*? Isaiah himself gives the answer in chapter 11:10-12, in terms of **the Root of Jesse**. That's ultimately Jesus, who stands so big in Scripture that he's both the 'root' (the ancestor) and the 'offspring' (the descendant) of Jesse's son, King David (Revelation 22:16). His rule runs both backwards and forwards across the whole of the Bible.

Here's a kingly, a Messianic standard. A standard is a symbol of **war** – in this case a spiritual conflict. It's also a symbol of **unity** – Christ crucified ('lifted up') draws people from every quarter (John 3:14). Further, it's a symbol of **conquest**. Evil *must* give way before the preaching of the Cross (Colossians 2:15). Lastly, this standard is a symbol of **direction**. Together we are following the rider on the White Horse (Revelation 19:11-16). The cry is 'Forward!'

Evil *must* give way before the preaching of the Cross.

12. A sense of history

The Lord is slow to anger and great in power; the Lord will not leave the guilty unpunished *(Nahum 1:3)*.

Just near the Iraqi city of Mosul – so much a scene of modern conflict – is a little mound called *Tell Kuyunjik*, 'the mound of many sheep', around which the whole prophecy of Nahum revolves. *Tell Kuyunjik* marks the spot where there had once existed the world's greatest capital city, Nineveh. In August 612 BC it was reduced to rubble by a combined assault of Babylonians, Scythians and Medes.

Fortress Nineveh represented Assyria's mighty war machine, and God's oppressed people cried out for retribution. But God is 'slow to anger' – too slow for some! Nearly 100 years earlier, the prophet Jonah had warned Nineveh of impending destruction, and as a result the entire city had repented, from the king downwards.

But now the shadows of judgment had lengthened, and the book of Nahum presents one of the great 'At lasts' of history. Jonah had highlighted the **mercy** of God; Nahum now emphasised his **severity**. Longfellow's translation of the poem *Retribution* strikes a chord here:

> **Though the mills of God grind slowly,**
> **yet they grind exceeding small.**

Get a sense of history from the Bible! That way, it's possible to see the rise and fall of unprincipled regimes through the binoculars of the on-going rule and kingdom of God.

Get a sense of history from the Bible!

13. Still thirsty?

What must I do to inherit eternal life? *(Luke 18:18).*

Lord Byron, the poet of the 18th and 19th centuries, set his heart on obtaining every experience going. BBC Television made a film, portraying his extremes. But he described himself in these words:

> *Drank every cup of joy, heard every trump of fame; drank early, deeply drank; drank draughts which common millions might have drunk. **Then died of thirst, because there was no more to drink.***

Here in Luke is a young man who drank *early* – and it wasn't satisfying him. He reads the gossip columns – about another young man whose speciality is eternal life! He decides, as usual, to go to the top.

Easier said than done! '*Excuse me, is Jesus here?*'

'Jesus? Sorry, he left half an hour ago.... he's at a wedding in Cana.... Sorry, he's just taken a boat.... No, he's at Levi's place with half the Galilean underworld!'

By the time our hero tracks Jesus down he's on his knees in the dust, literally (Mark 10:17). A fine recruit! But no. The young man has a burden which he can't let go. In his case it happens to be wealth; the burden of **getting it** ... the burden of **keeping it** ... the burden of **parting with it**!

He goes away. He's done a Lord Byron. The thirst remains.

The young man had a burden which he couldn't let go.

14. Model Christ

....that you might have him back for good – no longer as a slave, but better than a slave, as a dear brother *(Philemon 15, 16)*.

Slaves.....How was the Christian Gospel ever to overturn this massive system? Five times Paul refers to his *own* chains in this one-chapter letter to his Christian friend Philemon. Should he have advised the Christian slaves to organise a strike? To rise up in revolt against their Roman masters?

But to do that would have been to reduce Christ to the level of a mere Spartacus or Karl Marx. The Christians did something more revolutionary still. Within their own fellowship, they simply ignored the slave-master classifications *and treated them as though they didn't exist.*

Philemon had a slave, Onesimus, who had run away, met Paul in prison, become a Christian, and was now returning. 'Take him back', writes Paul to Philemon, 'but as a brother. **You be the first to model this!'**

Paul's letter was like a time-bomb, quietly ticking away in the heart of the Roman empire. Its time would come. What issues are **you** concerned about today? The spread of Pornography? Then see there's none in your own home. Racism? Then model the way of Christ *yourself.* The best revolutions start with just one person.

The best revolutions can start with just one person.

15. Wake up!

The hour has come for you to wake up from your slumber
(Romans 13:11).

Sixteen hundred years ago a classical scholar called Jerome dreamt that he'd died, and reached the gates of heaven. The gatekeeper spoke to him:

'Who are you?'

'Christianus sum', replied Jerome. 'I'm a Christian!'

'*No!*' retorted the gatekeeper. You're not a Christian – you're a Ciceronian! Here we judge people by what they were *most* when they were living on earth. And you did nothing but study the works of Cicero. So you're not a Christian, but a Ciceronian. You can't come in. Sorry!'

And Jerome woke up with a start, and made his resolve: 'First and foremost I will be a Christian'.

Then Jerome bent his scholastic ability into producing a translation of the Bible for the whole of Europe. It became known as the Vulgate version. It lasted for a thousand years – and united our culture right across Europe.

Take Christianity and the Bible out of Europe – and all that we're left with is a bunch of squabbling competing Barbarian tribes – which is roughly what we are today. It's time that some of us woke up again, like Jerome.

It's time that some of us woke up again.

16. Come alive!

Wake up, O sleeper, rise from the dead, and Christ will shine on you *(Ephesians 5:14).*

Yes, it was a little pop song that was going around the churches of the north Mediterranean, way back in about 60 AD, and the apostle Paul quotes from it.

At one point Paul and his fellow-preacher Silas were in jail and were singing songs at midnight (Acts 16:25). I can't help wondering whether the song of the locals popped into their minds:

> **Wake up, O sleeper,**
> **Rise from the dead,**
> **And Christ will shine on you.**

The pop song that got into the Bible! But is it any good trying to preach a **dead** person into life? Well, many of us are doing it today! Millions of us were once dead, as far as our awareness of Christ and eternity were concerned. Then something happened; someone spoke the message of Jesus to us; our spirits stirred and we woke up from the sleep of spiritual death.

As Charles Wesley put it in his hymn, **I woke, the dungeon flamed with light**. A thought for the week: Wake up to the Bible! Wake up to Prayer! Wake up to the church! *Come alive* to the wake-up call of Jesus Christ!

Come alive to the wake-up call of Jesus Christ!

17. The bright Morning Star

I am the Root and the Offspring of David, and the bright Morning Star *(Revelation 22:16)*.

If you've got a strong view of the future, you can be sure that the present will make plenty of sense ... but not otherwise! Here Jesus is speaking to the world on the last page of the Bible. See Him as:

The star of the Messiah
'... the Root and the Offspring of David' ... the kingly, messianic line. Jesus is not only the descendant ('Offspring') of David, but also the Ancestor ('Root')! Jesus is the all-time Ruler, from the very beginning.

The star of the millennium
This was a Jewish hope, of a future golden age. *A star shall come forth out of Jacob, and a sceptre shall rise out of Israel* (Numbers 24:17). The prophecy was fulfilled at the birth of Jesus – the Morning Star that would herald the dawn of the true New Age!

The star of mission and appeal
Our Bible sentence continues, *The Spirit and the Bride say 'Come!'* There is a joint appeal here. The Church ('the bride') is to issue it, in the power of the Spirit.

That has to be us – in our own generation! Provided that we possess the reality of 2 Peter 1:19 that describes the Christian experience when 'the morning star rises in your hearts'.

May the morning star rise in your heart today.

18. Are you giving for God?

I will not offer to the Lord my God that which cost me nothing
(2 Samuel 24:24).

King David had the God-given idea of building an altar on the threshing floor of a Jebusite farmer, Araunah. 'Just take it!' says Araunah. But David insists on paying the full market price. Here is a meeting of two generous spirits – an offering to God is no offering unless it costs!

Giving is something you can do jointly

Joint giving is dramatic. Mention a sum to me on my own, and I can wilt. But enthuse a bunch of people each to contribute the daily equivalent of a double-bacon cheeseburger – and ... well it could look attainable! Provided we're agreed that we're doing it together.

Giving is something you can do strategically

They had it all thought out. It started small – but Araunah's little threshing floor was to be the centre-point of the future mighty Temple of Solomon! (1 Chronicles 22:1). Great exploits will never be done if donors are still locked into the 'loose change' mindset of *tipping* only.

Giving is something you can do cheerfully

The two figures, king and farmer, vie with each other in their desire to give to God. *Are you doing this, for God and his church?* In a tax-effective way? Look back on what the Gospel has done for you, and you'll find you want to! Starting today....

Are you giving, for God and his church?

19. Go and wash

Go and wash ... and you shall be clean *(2 Kings 5:10 RSV).*

Disease and death ... the great levellers. Naaman was a five-star Syrian general with leprosy – on the same level as anybody else with a condition for which there was no apparent cure. No cure? Well, there was. But it had to be done God's way.

God's remedy is always humbling
It was a servant girl in the Naaman household who spoke of Elisha, the mighty Israelite prophet. A trip is undertaken, in hope of a cure. But on Naaman's arrival, accompanied by a full-dress parade, Elisha won't even come to the door. A prescription is handed out – *take a dip, in pint-sized, muddy Jordan river!* What? Naaman explodes.

God's cure is always simple
The general's aides calm him down, and the story has a happy ending. So, no special treatment for the great! The Gospel remedy for a world in alienation from its Creator is the same for one and all – *go and wash!*

God's cure is always free
Yes, we've moved onto the deepest of all human conditions, the need to be clean from our *sins*. It cost God the death of Christ his Son, to provide a remedy. But the fee for us is nothing. Provided we go to the one place where forgiveness can be found. Go to the Cross. Go and wash! *Now!*

Go and wash ... and you shall be clean.

20. The foolish message of the cross

For the message of the cross is foolishness to those who are perishing, but to us who are being saved it is the power of God *(1 Corinthians 1:18).*

How do *you* see the cross? It depends on which side of it you are standing.

The cross – foolishness or wisdom?
To the citizens of Corinth, the cross was a piece of foolishness – the Greek word used is *moron*. The Greeks were looking for a credible world-view, but today Plato is specialist reading for the esoteric few, while John's Gospel has led millions of people to the cross – and to peace with God. *On which side of the cross are YOU standing?*

The cross – weakness or strength?
To the apostle Paul's Jewish contemporaries, a crucified leader was a total disgrace! What they were interested in was *power* in life. They couldn't see what millions later saw – that Christ's death deals with human guilt and even death itself! *On which side of the cross are YOU standing?*

The cross – offence or essence?
What followers of Christ find is both 'wisdom' *and* 'power' – in one and the same person. His saving death is the key. Whether this means nothing to you, or everything that you ever hoped for, depends on your answer to a simple question: *On which side of the cross are YOU standing?*

On which side of the cross are YOU standing?

21. Suffering

Through many tribulations we must enter the kingdom of God
(Acts 14:22 RSV).

These words of Barnabas and Paul are the opposite of what we sometimes hear – that a true believer can expect full health, a topped-up bank balance and prospects of promotion. If this really was so, we could expect a flock of *customers* in the church, rather than disciples!

'Tribulation'
The Greek word is thlipsis – which refers to confining, squeezing pressure. Jesus promised that 'in the world you will have persecution'. Do we teach new believers this, from day one? We should. They will not be turned off – not if they have already been attracted by the magnetism of Christ.

'Must'
We should treat adversity as part of Christian living – first, because we follow Christ, who was himself subjected to opposition (Mark 8:31-34); and secondly because through adversity faith grows (1 Peter 1:6, 7).

'Enter'
Most people see trouble as a dead-end. The Bible regards it as a way *out* into progress and strength (Romans 5:3, 4) – the very life of the kingdom!

The kingdom of God
The term describes the rule that God exercises through Christ the appointed King, in the lives of his subjects world-wide. In spare moments this week, look up 2 Timothy 2:12, 1 Peter 4:13 and Revelation 1:9, and you will see that suffering is a *basic* part of Christian spirituality.

Suffering is a basic part of Christian spirituality.

22. Pray with expectation

After they prayed, the place where they were meeting was shaken. And they were all filled with the Holy Spirit and spoke the word of God boldly *(Acts 4:31).*

Praying together ... to what extent is it happening? Do the British Cabinet meetings begin with prayer, as Parliament does every day? They need to! For as Jacques Ellul once wrote, 'It is prayer, and prayer alone, that can make history'.

Years ago, my own father, Cecil Bewes, served on the British Government's *Fairn Commission* – set up as part of the process that paved the way for Kenya's independence. And Dad encouraged the others on the commission to begin the daily meetings with prayer *together*.

And why not? They practised it in the early church, and things happened! We can expect things to happen if we pray.

Whatever happened to the church Prayer Meeting across the country ... *when nothing else in the church is arranged on the same day* – so that all the church officers, council, youth and organisation leaders, and general membership can meet for prayer ... and expect the place to be shaken up a bit? Of course it takes some doing to get it started.

Coming to the prayer gathering?

Oh ... er – you mean singing, praise sessions, testimonies and reports?

No. It's really for prayer that we meet. We intercede. It's hard work. But that's where the action is!

Let's get combined prayer resurrected again. *Starting with the Cabinet?*

Let's get combined prayer resurrected again.

23. Faith in unexpected places

By faith Rahab the harlot did not perish with those who were disobedient, because she had given friendly welcome to the spies *(Hebrews 11:31 RSV).*

At a little Asian shop called *Fido's Bar*, in the dusty Kenyan town of Muranga, we once bought – of all unlikely things – a Santa Claus outfit. How did it come to be there, right by the equator? Well ... the presence of Rahab's name among the heroes of faith raises a similar question.

An unexpected ally in hostile territory
You'll find Rahab in the run-up to the Battle of Jericho in Joshua chapter 2. The whole success of the operation was due to the presence and co-operation of this prostitute with the plan of God for his people.

An unexpected faith in a heathen environment
Yes, she had faith, if you look up Joshua 2:9-11, and James 2:25. Is that hard to accept? The Jewish historian Josephus tried to tone Rahab down to 'a tavern-keeper'! But no, God can choose to bless and use a prostitute.

An unexpected ancestor in the royal line
Rahab even gets listed in Matthew 1:5 – as a distant ancestor of Christ! No one is ruled out for God's service. For her faith, Rahab was to be remembered long after Jericho was gone. Or Fido's Bar for that matter.

No one is ruled out for God's service.

24. Seize the day

From the days of John the Baptist until now the kingdom of heaven has suffered violence, and men of violence take it by force *(Matthew 11:12 RSV).*

As people surged around the carpenter-preacher, he was emphasising that when opportunity knocks, it's the eager who break through and win. Not with *physical* violence, so much as with spiritual fervour. Why is this so?

Because the difficulties are so many

There was so much to hamper those who wanted to get to Jesus! Take the woman with the haemorrhage who had to force her way through the crowd to touch the edge of his clothes and obtain healing. Or the paralysed man who had to be let through the roof. Or blind Bartimaeus the born loser, who had to shout for a hearing.

Because the possibilities are so great

The Roman centurion and his dying servant, Jairus and his ailing daughter, Nicodemus and his desperation for an interview with Jesus. Such people recognised that the tide was in, with the coming of Jesus – and took action!

Because the opportunities are so fleeting

The tide flows in – and then *out* once more. Zacchaeus, up his tree, took his chance, then and there in Jericho. Jesus never came that way again.

The door of spiritual opportunity is marked '*push*'. One day it will close.

The door of spiritual opportunity is marked '*push*'.

25. All is ours in Christ

For all things are yours, whether Paul or Apollos or Cephas or the world or life or death or the present or the future, all are yours; and you are Christ's , and Christ is God's *(1 Corinthians 3:21-23 RSV).*

Here the Corinthian believers had become split into human-centred factions – some claiming to belong to the apostle Paul's group, others to that of Apollos, or Peter (Cephas). But Paul turns their immature language around on them with his marvellous argument.

'You say that *you* belong to *them?* Don't you realise that *they* belong to *you?* In fact, if you belong to Christ, all things are yours'. The reasoning was that Christ has everything; thus the individual who belongs to Him possesses all things with Him – including those very ministers that we may think we belong to. The ministers belong to the church, not the church to the ministers. *And everything else in the universe belongs to the church!*

Far more than anyone else, Christian believers *know* their way around this world. Because of Christ it is no longer a puzzle. He has it all, and we are his and – in a final flourish – we learn that He is God's. That last phrase is vital – in belonging to Christ we have not joined yet one more human group. No, He is part of the very *Godhead.* All, all is ours.

If you belong to Christ, all things are yours.

26. Live to give

You go one way, and I'll go the other' *(Genesis 13:9 GNB).*

Sir John Laing, whose family business achieved international fame for integrity and skill in the building industry, was – as a Christian – giving away a great deal of his fortune as early as the 1940s; many were the new churches that owed their existence to his generosity. Millions of pounds passed through his hands. When he finally died, in his ninety-ninth year, his net personal estate amounted to £371. He had practised generosity all his life.

Perhaps he had learnt some of it from Abraham, who always sat lightly on his possessions – comparing favourably in this respect with his nephew Lot. The contrast was not between a saint and a sinner. It was more subtle than that. Genesis 13 presents us with a contrast between the advanced believer and the person who is content with an easy faith.

The test came when there was insufficient land to accommodate both families. The older man generously gave way: 'You go one way, and I'll go the other'. Lot immediately opted for the fertile Jordan valley. But Abraham's was the better attitude. From him we learn lessons about faith – its **flexibility**, its **generosity**, and its ultimate **prosperity**. Look up later this week Genesis 13:14, 15, and you'll see what Abraham's reward was.

Are you content with an easy faith?

27. Spiritual famine

I will send a famine through the land – not a famine of food or a thirst for water, but a famine of hearing the words of the Lord *(Amos 8:11).*

A famine of this kind doesn't happen fast; it's the relentless outworking of a general caving in to the ways of unbelief. This was the concern of a dusty little preaching farmer from Tekoa, 2,700 years ago.

His message still packs a punch – for vast tracts of the world today. **If you throw over your spiritual heritage of the past, God Himself will see to it that you are judged.** Your culture will fall apart, people will 'stagger' around in their discontent, unhappy, but not even knowing *why* they are unhappy (Amos 8:12, 13). You will be deprived of the very things that had undergirded you in the past; the Bible, prayer, the Christian Sunday, the ethical and moral principles that once had held you. All gone. And famine will set in – of the things for which the human spirit most craves.

The way back? *Begin with the church.* Get those ministers and clergy preaching their way through the Bible again. One Bible teaching church in every town – *just one* is enough! And back to the Bible ourselves. Daily. To quote Luis Palau, 'It's either back to the Bible, or back to the Jungle'.

It's either back to the Bible, or back to the Jungle.

28. Martha or Mary?

But only one thing is needed. Mary has chosen what is better, and it will not be taken away from her *(Luke 10:42).*

Think of any big social event where you were to meet with a celebrity. Years later, could you remember what food you ate? Probably not! But we needn't slam Martha, of this Bible story, *too* much – they would all have remembered the food if it had been rancid. Even so, when Jesus said that Mary, the other sister, had chosen 'that good *portion*' by sitting at His feet and listening, the word in the Greek New Testament is ambiguous; it could refer to the course of a meal.

It was as though Jesus was speaking playfully. **Martha, Martha ... all these dishes! But let's not deprive Mary of today's special dish!** *The one vital thing for the follower of Jesus is to hear and take in His words:*

We are to present ourselves ultimately, not as workers, but as disciples. To be an effective Martha, you need to be a Mary as well!

We are to focus, not on the many things, but on the one thing – that is, spending time in the presence of Jesus Christ.

We are to model ourselves, not on each other, but on Christ. We're not to be imitators of Martha, Mary or anybody else, but Christ alone.

Be imitators of Christ alone.

29. Who is in control?

**The Lord opened her heart.... At that moment the spirit left her....
The jailor woke up** *(Acts 16:14, 18, 27).*

A businesswoman, a fortune-teller and the town jailor – three vivid
conversion stories from the frontier Roman colony city of Philippi.
The issue in each cameo comes as a question: *Who controls?*

'In control' (Acts 16:13-15)
Lydia – a God-fearer in her own way, a capable business dealer in
purple cloth, she seemed thoroughly 'in control' of her life and
destiny. But as the apostle Paul explained Christ's good news there
by the riverside, the control passed, from herself to Christ – who
had 'opened her heart'.

'Under control' (Acts 16:16-18)
This was more sinister. The fortune-teller was 'under' control of the
wrong kind – first of an evil spirit; secondly of her human exploiters.
By the power of Christ's name she is freed – and again, the control
changes.

'Out of control' (Acts 16:19-40)
The girl's exploiters take out their rage on Paul and Silas – who
end up in jail. Then the earthquake hits – and the prison cracks
open! With control gone, the jailor is suicidal – but then and there,
Paul leads him to Christ. The story ends with Paul and Silas joining
Europe's first newly-formed house group – back at Lydia's house!
Who controls? That's the issue.

Who controls? That's the issue.

30. Christ our Rock

For their rock is not like our Rock, as even our enemies concede
(Deuteronomy 32:31).

Here is one of the greatest speeches of history, given by Moses as he hands over Israel's leadership to Joshua. He's warning God's people against ever lowering their standards. The idolatry and child-sacrifice of the surrounding nations was so totally inferior to Israel's durable Rock – the Rock of Monotheism, of the Law, of the Covenant and of Worship; why, he maintains, even their enemies conceded this point!

Here was a Rock which, in a strange way, wasn't a mere static thing, out there in the wilderness. It 'followed' them, because this Rock was more an idea than a pile, more a *relationship* than a religion, even. Ultimately it was a *person* – no less than the Second Person of the Trinity, Christ Himself (1 Corinthians 10:1-4).

What foundation can compare with this? Who was more **credible**, Moses, or his adverssary, Pharoah of Egypt? Who was more **durable**, Daniel the prophet or his counterpart Nebuchadnezzar – who finally acknowledged the superiority of Daniel's God? Who was more **stable**, John the Baptist or Herod? Keep going ... history supplies the answers!

Here is a Rock that isn't dependent on the job market, health fluctuations or the political climate. *But don't wait for a crisis to strike*. Put it – or rather Him – to the test *now!*

Put Christ your rock to the test now!

31. Fool for Christ

I made a fool of myself, but you drove me to it *(2 Corinthians 12:11).*

Paul had been fighting for the soul of a church led astray by power-mad, self-made 'apostles', who were obsessed with miracles. So Paul had joined the triumphalist boasting game – showing that if the Christian life really was a miraculous balloon ride, then he could outdo the lot of them! Why, he had been caught up to the third heaven (2 Corinthians 12:1-4) – though if we are to understand Paul properly, the real 'wonders' that gave substance to his leadership were the trials and hardships listed in chapter 11:21-33. The whole of 1 and 2 Corinthians is about *power through weakness – with the saving death of Christ at the centre.*

So leave the power trip behind; it's madness to boast; Paul had simply been matching the folly of the counterfeit apostles with his own 'folly'. But back to **sanity**, and to proper **ministry**, and back to **maturity**.

Once people have decided that they have *moved on* from the centrality of the cross, have got tired of the old paths, it's not easy to come back to 'boring' old Bible study again! But come back we must, to the *real* Christian life, even if, as in Paul's case, you have to fight folly – with folly!

Come back to the REAL Christian life!

32. God's great sieve

For I will give the command and I will shake the house of Israel among all the nations, as grain is shaken in a sieve, and not a pebble will reach the ground *(Amos 9:9).*

Years ago in my educational gap year I decided – partly as a preparation for Christian ministry – to spend twelve months working on the shop floor of a great biscuit factory in London. To this day I couldn't tell you how a biscuit is actually *made*; my job was, for the most part, confined to managing a machine that shook continuously.

It was a very large sieve. I was required to separate and sieve out the impurities from the sugar that went into the biscuits. Nothing impure must get through. All sorts of bits and pieces ended up on the top of my sieve. One day I even sieved out a little mouse. Well, it wouldn't have been too good if it had got mixed in with the custard creams.

A basic process ... and so it is in God's shaking up of all history – the separation of the good from the evil, the sheep from the goats, the repentant from the rebels. The final issue is, *What did you do with Jesus, who suffered rejection instead of you?* Look up Hebrews 12:26, 27.

What did you do with Jesus?

33. Triumph and disaster

I have learned, in whatsoever state I am, therewith to be content.
I know both how to be abased, and I know how to abound
(Philippians 4:11,12 KJV).

These words remind me of the Wimbledon tennis! I've been there so many times; I've even played there as a schoolboy junior. I've sold ices at Wimbledon, queued all night on the pavement, the lot!

Once, I was privileged to be with Chris Gorringe, then Wimbledon's Chief Executive. He was the one who, on Finals Day, would hand the champion's trophy to the Duchess of Kent before she presented it to the winner on the Centre Court. I was shown everything – including the lines from Kipling that are inscribed over the entrance to the Centre Court:

> **If you can meet with Triumph and Disaster**
> **And treat those two impostors just the same**

That's the philosophy of the apostle Paul in prison. It's not about 'being a good loser'! It's about your whole attitude to life and its countless tensions. It looks like a downer for Paul, but because he is 'content' *in Christ*, he is actually winning. Through his prison correspondence (which became part of the Bible) he's learnt to convert a prison cell into a broadcasting studio for the world!

It's Christ who gives us that. Paul 'learnt' it. And so can we all.

Paul learnt contentment, and so can we.

34. Persecution

In the present case I advise you: Leave these men alone! Let them go! For if their purpose or activity is of human origin, it will fail. But if it is from God, you will not be able to stop these men; you will only find yourselves fighting against God' *(Acts 5:38, 39).*

Wise, wise Gamaliel! One of the top leaders in the religious governing body of the day, he knew his history. Here in the book of Acts, the people who were called Christians were growing in numbers. They posed a threat to the established institutions in Jerusalem. What was to be done?

Wipe 'em out! That was the consensus among the authorities. Gamaliel alone disagreed. He'd seen other movements arise, only to disappear eventually (Acts 5:34-39).

How can the authorities in any society guarantee both the preservation and growth of the Christian church? Answer: *persecute it*. It is amazing that those countries today that are bent on banning the Bible and containing the church haven't learnt from history. Not that we invite pressurising tactics against us, or our Christian sisters and brothers who face imprisonment and martyrdom today. But pressure makes the church even tougher than before. You can't fight Jesus.

The modern historian T.R. Glover wrote, *The final disappearance of Christianity has been prophesied so often as to be no longer interesting.*

The final disappearance of Christianity has been prophesied so often as to be no longer interesting.

35. Lessons from Leviticus

Aaron's sons the priests shall bring the blood and sprinkle it against the altar on all sides at the entrance to the Tent of Meeting *(Leviticus 1:5).*

Must we bother with Leviticus? All that about blood sacrifice? In our fellowship studies, can't we go straight to Jesus in the New Testament?

The answer is 'Sure – if you're helping new Christians'. Jesus dying for our sins; that's all they need. But even at that stage questions may arise: 'Why did Jesus see Himself as a *sacrifice?*' Answer: 'Look at Leviticus!'

1. A foundational book
There is a progression in the early books of the Bible. Genesis presents us with a **ruined race**. Exodus introduces us to a **redeemed people**. And Leviticus develops the theme of a **holy nation**. Leviticus provides us with God's original prototype model for our forgiveness and purification.

2. An educational book
Sprinkling ... blood ... altars – how repelling! Yet in contrast to the Greek and other ancient civilisations, human sacrifice played no part in God's order; a *substitute* sacrifice had to be found. The lesson was, sin mattered!

3. A Christological book
The different ancient sacrifices are summarised in Leviticus 7:37. They paved the way for *Christ*. Take time to look up 1 Peter 1:18-19. Ultimately, Leviticus is all about Jesus. Know that as you start to read it!

Leviticus is all about Jesus!

36. Wait till harvest

Let both grow together until the harvest *(Matthew 13:30).*

My uncle Keith, frying an onion one day, couldn't understand why he became so ill. But what he'd cooked and eaten was a daffodil bulb.

What to do, when alien produce gets mixed in with the genuine? So ran Jesus' story of the farmer, whose enemy sowed weeds in among his wheat (Matthew 13:24-30). A mixed crop? Should they pull up the weeds?

'Maybe *not*,' was the verdict, 'in case you pull up the wheat as well. Wait till harvest. Then 'll be the time to sort out the weeds and burn them'.

1. Jesus is teaching about the state of the world
The farmer's field is like the world. It's a good world, but evil, error and wrong-doing are all mixed in, growing alongside. Can we understand?

2. Jesus is teaching about the character of Christian work
Patience is called for. How large the weeds grow! *But Christ's work is growing too.* His is the only really productive work. Are you involved?

3. Jesus is teaching about the climax of history
The harvest is the final judgment. There's an end coming! The counterfeit is all going to be bundled up and burnt. The genuine? It'll be kept for God.

The genuine will be kept for God.

37. Get the centre right

Seek ye first the kingdom of God and his righteousness, and all these things will be added unto you *(Matthew 6:33 KJV)*.

Here is Jesus, in the most influential sermon ever given. But the Sermon on the Mount isn't an entrance exam, or a piece of therapy – on the level of *How to be Happy or How to Succeed at being Yourself.*

Here are no trite tips on life. Jesus is presenting a radical manifesto of the life that is expected from members of his kingdom. **And it's all about the centre**. This didn't go down well with the Pharisees who were listening. They could only concentrate on the circumference; their robes and tassels, their oratorical public prayers and their ostentatious fasting. But they'd missed out on the heart, on the centre of the kingdom – which is the rule of Jesus Himself as King in people's lives.

The other people who miss out, said Jesus, are the people of this world, who worry constantly about the circumference – what to wear, what to eat, where to live. It's everywhere today; the latest Versace fashions, the finest wines, the most effective cosmetic surgery. Today's magazines say it all; *just living ... to live* – while neglecting the small matter of life itself.

Get the centre right, says the world's greatest teacher, and the rest will fit in. Let Jesus and His word act as the rudder for the start of every day!

Let Jesus and His word act as the rudder for the start of every day!

38. By faith Noah. . .

By faith Noah, when warned about things not yet seen, in holy fear built an ark to save his family. By his faith he condemned the world and became heir of the righteousness that comes by faith *(Hebrews 11:7).*

'*Fear*' and '*faith*' are not really contradictory. In holy fear Noah builds an ark, and by his faith he condemns the world, for 2 Peter 2:5 tells us that Noah was a preacher. How he preached!

Noah's message became embedded in our memory
There's not a society anywhere that is unaware of the Flood. We don't have to explain *which* Flood. It's stamped upon our global consciousness.

Noah's message became embodied in our theology
From Noah we learn that God always warns. Lot warned Sodom. Moses warned Pharaoh. Jeremiah warned Judah. Jonah warned Nineveh. But Noah is primary here; he was foundational, because he warned *the world!*

Noah's message became embossed on our testimony
Ignore God, and all our neat plans are likely to end up as watery pulp. It was Jesus who took Noah as His model of teaching about the end times. When you have time this week, look up Matthew 24:37, and you'll see!

God always warns.

39. Saving faith

Were not all ten cleansed? Where are the other nine? *(Luke 17:17).*

The real beneficiary among the ten leprosy sufferers healed by Jesus, was the one who returned to give thanks. Three sentences stand out:

They stood at a distance
These ten were officially outcasts – and they included an alien Samaritan in their number. Solidarity in the face of a crisis can bring the deadliest of enemies together. In the Mozambique flood of 2000, an Anglican archdeacon found himself sharing a tree with a cobra – for four days!

He threw himself at Jesus' feet
It was, as the ten went at Jesus' command to present themselves before the priest for official clearance, that they were healed. A fine and even beautiful story! But there's more. It's the alien Samaritan alone who returned to Jesus in true faith and thanksgiving. *His was a saving faith.*

Your faith has saved you
Yes, it's the *sozo* word in the Greek – 'saved'. All told, ten were 'cleansed' (v. 14). Only one was 'saved' (v. 19). In a sense those other nine remained 'at a distance' from Jesus. Only one obtained the true reality of a saving, personal faith in the Son of God. It changed him forever.

**The real beneficiary was the one
who returned to give thanks.**

40. Do not grumble

And do not grumble, as some of them did – and were killed by the destroying angel *(1 Corinthians 10:10).*

Even God can't be patient forever – when it comes to grumblers! Here is the apostle Paul, looking back on the history of God's people:

Grumbling – the diagnosis of a chronic disorder
You can't be praising God and grumbling at one and the same time! If you're a grumbler *something's wrong with you.* In church life, it's usually a summer complaint – and it acts like a contagious epidemic – beginning with just a very few, gathering together in 'Moaner's Corner'.

Grumbling – the description of the inactive backliner
Come to Israel's front line in a battle with the Amalakites. 'How's the battle going?' you ask. 'Oh, okay', comes the reply. 'We've lost a quarter of the platoon – but we can hold this hill. We can cope!'

Then to the backline. 'How's it going?' 'Oh, terrible! My tent leaks. And we had manna again for breakfast'. *Are you a frontliner or a backliner?*

Grumbling – the definition of spiritual rebellion
Ultimately sin is a grumbling against God (Exodus 16:8). It's lined up in 1 Corinthians 10 along with idolatry and sexual immorality! The antidote? *Learn from the past; don't hanker for it. Count your blessings; don't take them for granted. Get onto the front line and don't be a spectator.*

Are you a frontliner or a backliner?

41. Daniel

And Daniel remained there until the first year of King Cyrus
(Daniel 1:21).

Here's a young Hebrew – a college student – taken captive along with thousands of others 2,600 years ago. Out there in alien Babylon, along with his friends, Shadrach, Meshak and Abednego, he is going not only to survive in his faith, but to win. He does it by dint of his godly character:

Daniel resolved (v. 8)
He and his friends had to start somewhere in their fight for integrity – so they begin on the food front. 'No palace food, thanks; it's too defiling. Stick us on a high fibre diet!' And they won through. *What is your issue?*

Daniel understood'(v. 17)
Somehow the famous four were able to take on the dream and vision culture of the Babylonians – and then prove the superiority of their own belief-system. We can do it too – but only if we are thorough-going students of the Word of God. Otherwise we cave in like everyone else.

Daniel remained'(v. 21)
It was character that saw Daniel through each repressive regime, and right through to the end of the Jewish exile – and beyond. 'Character', said D.L. Moody, 'is worth more than money. Character is worth more than anything else in the wide world'.

How can a pagan regime be outlasted? The answer lies right here.

**Character is worth more than
anything else in the wide world.**

42. Redeeming the time

Redeeming the time, because the days are evil *(Ephesians 5:16).*

The nervous fiddling with the mobile phone, the daily blizzard of E-mails – whatever happened to time? Why, even in the laconic Australian outback, the advert reads, '*Ears Pierced – while U wait!*' How to win against Time?

Be creative in your use of time

Forget trying to account for every half-hour period of your day. Ask rather, What is my day *for*? King Alfred the Great divided every 24 hours into three; eight hours for sleep, recreation and meals; eight for public business, and eight for private study and devotion. And still he had time to beat the Danes, and make Britain a Christian country. Get the *main* plan right!

Be redemptive in your use of time

Set your own pace. Do you tick quickly or slowly? Are you an early morning lark, or a late-night owl? Are you steady and methodical, or an improviser? Work it out, and live accordingly. And secondly, *find your own space.* Space for work, sure, but also for dreaming dreams.

Be defensive in your use of time

Defensive, *because the days are evil.* Set up some defence mechanisms. As the philosopher La Maistre declared, 'I have so much to do that I must go to bed'. The best defence of all is time spent with God. Jesus did so with His heavenly Father (Mark 1:35). We can do that. Let's start today.

The best defence of all is time spent with God.

43. Here comes the Christ!

At that time if anyone says to you, 'Look, here is the Christ!' or 'There he is!' do not believe it *(Matthew 24:23).*

Years ago, when my parents were leading the work at Tonbridge Parish Church in Kent, they invited the famous pop singer, Cliff Richard, to come for a Sunday night guest service, complete with guitar.

They knew Cliff as a name, but my saintly mother had never seen him, not even on television. As various young men came and went to the Vicarage that afternoon, my mum would wonder, 'Is that the one? ... Or that?... How will I recognise him when he comes?

But eventually, when a party of visitors clambered out of a Rolls Royce and walked up the Vicarage path, in a protective shield around the central figure, my mother was emphatic. 'When the real thing turned up at last', she said, 'there was absolutely no mistaking which one was Cliff Richard!'

So it will be with the return of Jesus Christ at the end of history. True, people over the centuries have made claims that they were the expected Christ, but the saints were not taken in. When He returns, bodily, visibly, publicly and as universal Judge, no one, no one at all is going to say, '*Who's that?*' There will be instant recognition.

When He returns, there will be instant recognition.

44. False prophets

I will cut off from this place every remnant of Baal, the names of the pagan and the idolatrous priests – those who bow down on the housetops to worship the starry host *(Zephaniah 1:4)*.

Zephaniah, aged about twenty, was the first of a new line of prophets. After him would come Jeremiah and others. The fact was, that since the mighty Isaiah, *there had been no prophetic voice in Judah for some seventy years.*

In that time there had been some slippage! Now it was 627 BC, and here was a new voice, and a new opportunity. There's no time to lose as the young Zephaniah thunders out his message of judgment on God's people.

And the priests would be singled out first! Part of the judgment was that their very *names* would be blotted out. Christian – does it worry you when certain leaders in the church teach falsehood, and gain a following?

It is a right concern....*but they won't last.* It's only a matter of time. Give it five, ten years, and their books will end up in the *Oxfam* shops. People will scratch their heads and say, 'Who was it who taught all that stuff?' They will have passed into the oblivion of our collective forgetfulness. Their names will have been cut off.

False prophets won't last!

45. Samuel

When Samuel spoke, all Israel listened *(1 Samuel 3:21 GNB).*

Samuel comes into the story of Israel to close off the unprincipled era of the Judges, when authority in the land was at a low ebb, when people lived according to their own standards. It was a kind of spiritual famine. *'In those days the word of the Lord was rare'* (1 Samuel 3:1).

Samuel was about twelve when he was called, that dramatic night in Shiloh. He went to bed as a very young lay assistant to the priest Eli. By the morning he was a prophet. Before long everyone knew it!

There have been times, when the world seems to be in a long sleep; then a scholar like Wycliffe would wake up to the Bible, or martyrs like Latimer and Ridley would light a fire which was never to go out.

In Samuel's case, a growing recognition took hold of Israel again, as Samuel's message gained a hearing: *We've found ourselves again; God is among us, and He's speaking.*

God can do that **anywhere** – in a family, within a campus hall of residence, in a business house or bank, within a football team. It only takes one person – who is alive to God's call.

It only takes one person – who is alive to God's call.

46. This man is it!

See, this is getting us nowhere. Look how the whole world has gone after him! *(John 12:19).*

You can't stop Jesus. This was the conclusion arrived at by His enemies. The Jesus movement was beginning to roll – and they were in despair. 'This is getting us nowhere!' There is something about Christ's character and magnetic appeal that has universal appeal.

After all, by the end of today, some 100,000 more people across the world will have become followers of Jesus – that's the scale of the demographics. And by the end of this week, some 16 hundred new churches will have come into being – that weren't in existence last week! At Billy Graham's **Amsterdam 2000** congress, I met with a pastor from the Cameroon. They had just *one showing* of the 'Jesus' film in his area – that was enough to create a new church.

Are you signed up yet? Read John's Gospel if you need convincing. By the time you get to chapter 5, my hunch is that you'll be saying, 'This Man is *it*!' People can try stamping out the Jesus movement. They've been at it for centuries. But where has it got them? Better to come to terms with His love, His authority over darkness, death and despair – personally. You can't stop Jesus.

You can't stop Jesus.

47. Power from on high

You would have no power over me if it were not given to you from above *(John 19:11).*

The trial of Jesus had an element of power play about it. Who really had the power?

1. Raw power. In an attempt to win their way, the enemies of Jesus had relied on money bribes, lies, secrecy, torches and lanterns, blood, fists, sticks and nails. *Is that the way to win?* It gets a short-term result, but it's doomed to fail!

2. Vested power. Ultimately it was the religious interests that felt most threatened by Christ. In the clamour for blood, it was the revered leaders, who, for all their their God-talk, took the lead in having Jesus killed.

3. Token power. The enemies of Jesus knew how to manipulate the weakness of Pilate to their own ends. He was desperate to keep his job and he caved in, and handed Jesus over. He had no power at all – as Jesus had pointed out.

4. Silent power. It wasn't Pilate, but the silent Jesus, who in reality occupied the Judge's seat throughout. He had the control, and as resurrected and ascended king He still does, until the end of time.

Jesus has control – until the end of time.

48. Look for the signs

And let it be, when thou hearest the sound of a going in the tops of the mulberry trees, that then thou shalt bestir thyself; for then shall the Lord go out before thee... *(2 Samuel 5:24 KJV).*

In the old Gospel hymn *Blessed Assurance*, there is a line that runs, 'Watching and waiting, looking above....' That is precisely what King David was required to do at a particular crisis point. The sound of a stirring of the leaves in the treetops might have meant nothing to others, but David was alerted. He would take no steps without God.

Christian history is studded with examples. Noah was well prepared for the Flood, in a cynical unheeding society. Lot had to be alerted to the impending devastation of Sodom and Gomorrah (Genesis 19). Elijah was sensitive to the still small voice of God (1 Kings 19:12). And think of the Wesley brothers of the eighteenth century: they had to be stirred into wakefulness at Oxford – only then could they be used to stir slumbering Britain.

But don't leave it to the great ones of this earth! Let every day begin with prayer and the Bible. Learn to read heaven's signals of what is happening on our tormented planet – that way we can be stirred into meaningful action!

Learn to read heaven's signals!

49. Fear not!

Fear not, I am the first and the last and the living one; I died, and behold I am alive for evermore, and I have the keys of Death and Hades *(Revelation 1:17, 18 RSV).*

It was a nightmare time for Christians. The Roman emperor Domitian insisted on being worshipped as *Dominus et Deus* ('Lord and God'). Christian worship was forbidden, on pain of execution.

But the book of Revelation came into being around the year 95 AD, written down by Christ's disciple, John. The theme of these inspired visions was the triumph of Jesus over evil, Satan and death. As I have written in my book, '*The Stone that became a Mountain*' (Christian Focus Publications), **'To read the book of Revelation is to expose yourself to the sheer strength and momentum of the New Testament church, whose calling it was to show the world for all time how we outlive and outlast tyrannies.'**

Fear not. How often Jesus had spoken those words during His earthly ministry! Now at the outset of this wonderful prophecy, alive for ever from the grave and irradiated in glory, He reminds His followers for all time that the keys of the vital, the eternal issues, are safe in His hands. That being so, *nothing else matters.*

Fear not – the keys are safe in his hands.

50. God is on the throne

At once I was in the Spirit, and there before me was a throne in heaven with someone sitting on it *(Revelation 4:2).*

When the Ugandan dictator (*'President for Life'*) Idi Amin was being toppled from power in the 1970s, the end result looked in the balance – until he lost his centre, the capital Kampala. At that point the whole world knew that his next stop would be the border. Sure, he continued to defy and threaten his enemies from a mobile broadcasting transmitter, but his control was broken. His centre had gone.

When we read the book of Revelation, there are some terrifying passages within it. The powers of evil seem to be at work ceaselessly, in the world scene that Christ leads His followers of every age to expect. Satan and his allies appear everywhere, threatening, persecuting and killing.

Where is God all this time? Throughout all these visions, **He never leaves the throne**. That tells us everything we need to know; that the centre is intact and that goodness has the final say. As another Ugandan, Bishop Festo Kivengere – a contemporary of Amin – once observed in my presence, 'Satan can roar like a lion, but he has no authority to shake the throne on which Jesus is sitting'.

Satan has no authority to shake God's throne.

51. Who is worthy?

I wept and wept because no-one was found who was worthy to open the scroll or look inside *(Revelation 5:4).*

In the apostle John's words here, it's a little like the old fable of Cinderella: the kitchen girl, who could only become recognised as the rightful princess, if the celebrated glass slipper fitted her foot alone!

For here in the book of Revelation, John is looking at the destiny and history of the human race – depicted by a scroll with seven seals. The call goes out, **Is there anyone big enough for the title role of Interpreter of our existence, who can unravel the scroll and its secrets?**

Failure, abject failure. It's not for want of trying, but the many aspirants for the role all fail. Flawed in their own moral need, they are now in their graves. It's tragic, and John weeps. No one 'worthy' is found.

Except one. *Weep not,* comes the reassurance. In Revelation 1 it had been *Fear not.* This last book of all is packed with comfort for God's people. The Lamb of God, once slain but now alive for ever, comes onto the stage and opens the Scroll! Christ crucified is the explanation of all history, and makes sense of life. Has He done it for you?

Christ crucified is the explanation of all history.

52. The wrath of the Lamb

They called to the mountains and the rocks, 'Fall on us and hide us from the face of Him who sits on the throne and from the wrath of the Lamb!' *(Revelation 6:16).*

Whoever heard of a lamb that was wrathful? At the start of Jesus' earthly ministry, John the Baptist had identified Him as 'the Lamb of God, who takes away the sin of the world' (John 1:29). Christ's was to be a mission of love and self-sacrifice for the whole world. Now as the apostle John spells out from his vision 'what must soon take place', he forsees at the end of the age the cosmic shakings that will accompany the Last Judgment.

The day of Christ's return will be terrifying. No one, however great, will escape the coming wrath if they have rejected his salvation and ignored his claims. Kings, princes, generals, the rich, and the mighty will be alongside both slave and free, in their frantic attempts to hide among the caves and rocks, when the day comes (Revelation 6:15-17).

In every age, the upheavals of the world are like a warning klaxon horn: **Get ready; it will be worse on that day; repent, obey the Gospel and make peace now with the chosen Lamb of God, who died for you.**

**Make peace now with the chosen
Lamb of God, who died for you.**

53. He is here

Mine eyes have seen thy salvation *(Luke 2:30).*

The Greek epic, *The Iliad*, written around 700 BC, vividly tells the story of Agamemnon, leader of the Greek forces against Troy, and the placing of a sentinel to keep watch, year after year, for the beacon-signal that would signal that Troy had, at last, been taken.

After ten long years, the strategy of the famous Wooden Horse brought victory. The news blazed from hill to hill. '*Troy has fallen!*', the sentinel was informed, 'Your duty is done; the long wait is over. You are relieved!'

It was a similar situation affecting the devout Simeon, when Jesus was born. He really belonged to the old order, but – assured by God's Spirit that he wouldn't die until he'd seen *the Lord's Christ* (Luke 2:26) – he'd gone, day after day, to the temple courts, watching the mums and dads as they came to present their babies before God. Which *was* the baby?

Time passed by. Then one day Mary and Joseph walked in, holding the infant Jesus. It was like a beacon blaze. Release had come for God's watchman and *the waiting was over*. Read Luke 2:28-32, for Simeon's words of praise. Those who wait for *God's* moment will be rewarded!

Those who wait for *God's* moment will be rewarded!

54. Great days!

Forget the former things; do not dwell on the past. See; I am doing a new thing! Now it springs up; do you not perceive it? *(Isaiah 43:18, 19).*

I was buying myself some new shoes in Southport, a fine shopping town in England's Merseyside. 'I'd like them to be in exactly the same style as the shoes I'm wearing now', I explained to the shop lady.

'The same style?' she challenged. 'How dull!'

The one great thing with the actions of *God* is that they are never dull. God never repeats his wonders. That's not in his style. Here in our passage, the prophet has just referred to the deliverance, centuries earlier, of the Israelites through the Red Sea (Isaiah 43:16, 17).

'Forget all that!' comes the message now. 'That's in the past. *A new thing is about to happen.* And so it proved, in the momentous return of God's battered people from exile. 'Look ahead to the future!' was the emphasis.

I remember an old evangelical preacher, Llewellyn Roberts by name. He had been through some great eras. But he didn't live in the past. 'These are great days to be living in!' I heard him exclaim to a colleague. '*Great days!*' He was then well over eighty. That's the style; stay young!

Don't dwell on the past. Look ahead to the future!

55. A reassuring presence

My Presence will go with you, and I will give you rest *(Exodus 33:14).*

When one of our boys was to start travelling to his school by the London Underground, I went along with him for the first few rides; first sitting with him, then a few seats away, next at the far end of the compartment, and finally in the next door carriage – just as a reassuring presence!

Here now is Moses, facing not just a few weeks, but years of testing leadership. He puts his concern to the Lord, 'You have not let me know whom you will send with me' (Exodus 33:12).

The divine answer is relevant to every believer across time! *My Presence will go with you.* Who is this Presence? It has to be the pre-incarnate second Person of the Trinity. Although Moses cannot see the Father's face (v. 20), even so, *in this same chapter,* 'the Lord' is also said to 'speak with Moses, face to face, as a man speaks with his friend'. It's no mistake. Here is a firm Old Testament pointer to the truth of the Trinity. *Christ*, who makes the Father visible (John 1:18) would personally lead his people into the future (1 Corinthians 10:4). He'll do it for you, if you trust him.

Christ will lead you into the future.

56. Where two or three are gathered…

Let us not give up meeting together, as some are in the habit of doing, but let us encourage one another – and all the more as you see the Day approaching *(Hebrews 10:25).*

Yes, there's no time to waste! All that's needed in our towns and villages is to have a single church fellowship in place – just *one* – where the Bible is believed and taught, and where the members come together to pray, *and a whole locality can be affected.* Such is the power of God's holy Word. Such is the dynamic of prayer and Gospel worship!

If there are **enough** towns where a Bible witness exists, there comes into being the possibility of changing society, government and even a nation. Revivals have begun in this way.

But there must be agreement among the members: 'We are going to do this in our church together, right through the year. We'll be there every Sunday and bring our Bibles. *We'll never miss.* No Prayer Meeting, eh? Very well, we'll start one this week – if necessary in someone's home'.

It only takes two or three people of determination – and you'll have a swinging fellowship. And – in Matthew 18:20 – Christ promises to join you!

It only takes two or three people of determination.

57. Christ's sacrifice

He sacrificed for their sins once for all when he offered himself
(Hebrews 7:27).

At All Souls we had a staff colleague once called Diane Baird. She was to become a minister's wife in Belfast. On one occasion we persuaded her to represent the Christian faith at a business people's world convention on the continent of Europe. All belief systems had been invited to send a rep, and Diane was our choice. She did well. We were proud of her.

During it she found herself in friendly conversation with a leader from another religion. He was clad in colourful robes.

'The difference between you and me' said Diane, is a four-letter word!'

'Oh, really?' queried the man.

'Yes, definitely. It's obvious as we've talked that, with you, it's **DO**. "Do this ... undergo that ritual ... perform this observance" – for you it's all **DO**, if you're to gain eternal fulfilment. But', said Diane, 'with us who belong to Christ it's **D-O-N-E**. He's achieved for all of us what we could never have gained for ourselves – forgiveness, eternal life and a place in his eternal kingdom. He's done it all through his death on the Cross for the sins of the whole world. *Done* ... It's a four-letter word!

'*Done* ... It's a four-letter word!

58. You're more than a number!

Take a census of the whole Israelite community by their clans and families, listing everyone by name, one by one' *(Numbers 1:2).*

Yes, every individual is of significance when God is at work! This is the book of *Numbers*. Genesis presented the human race as a **ruined people**, after the Fall. Exodus introduced a **redeemed people**, from the slavery of Egypt. Leviticus developed the theme of a **holy people**. Now here is Numbers with its emphasis on a **pilgrim people**, on the journey to the Promised Land. Are you on God's present day list, by the way?

'Oh', you say, 'I'm a nothing person; I'm just an anonymous cypher – I can't count for anything.'

Don't be too sure. I've been typing since the age of eight. Earlier in my life the little @ key meant nothing to me. If I ever used it at all, it was to make a decorative border – it could have sighed that it was terribly under-used. *Not now!* World-wide, it's come into its own, on e-mails, and on websites by the million.

If we're part of God's pilgrim people, **God takes note of us**, 'name by name', and will use us. You have a role to play. Give it time; you're a key @ person!

You have a role to play.

59. Be different

If a man or woman wants to make a special vow, a vow of separation to the Lord as a Nazirite ... he must fulfil the vow he has made, according to the law of the Nazirite *(Numbers 6:2, 21).*

Athletes go into training. Students revise and concentrate for the exam. But what did you know of the Nazirites, 32 centuries ago?

It was all part of the training of God's ancient people as they travelled to their Promised Land. *Nazir* is the Hebrew for 'set apart'. A lay person – usually for a specific period of time – would set himself or herself apart, for a complete commitment to God. This would involve the taking of a vow and the adoption of a detailed and disciplined lifestyle.

Today's Christian – every Christian – is the modern counterpart. But there's a difference. 1. The Nazirite vow was for a limited group; *Christian commitment is for all.* 2. The Nazirite vow was for a limited period; *Christian commitment is for ever.* 3. The Nazirite vow demanded a limited ritual; *Christian commitment touches every part of life.*

Therefore come out from them and be separate, says the Lord. Touch no unclean thing, and I will receive you. I will be a Father to you *(2 Corinthians 6:17, 18).*

Therefore come out from them and be separate.

60. Memories

You deserted the Rock, who fathered you; you forgot the God who gave you birth *(Deuteronomy 32:18).*

A piece of music can do it, or an old photograph in a dust-laden album, or – as in the fable of Dick Whittington – the sound of London's Bow bells that recalled him to his duty. Suddenly, memories come rushing back, and you become integrated once more, and *operational.*

Memory is essential if we are to survive, and reach our destined goal. This was the issue facing Israel as Moses, in one of the most powerful orations of all history, recalled his people to their roots shortly before his death. **Israel was in danger of succumbing to a corporate memory loss.**

When that happens to any people – and it is happening right across the West at the present time – a crumbling process sets in. Politicians, media tycoons, playwrights, and certain 'historians' become selective with their research. Mistakes from the past, that could have been avoided, get repeated. Golden moments of creativity and spirituality (without which no nation can prosper) are conveniently skated over and forgotten. Mighty leaders are banished to the archives. As a society *forgets*, so it folds over.

Let's bone up on our past. We must *remember*, if we want to survive!

We must *remember*, if we want to survive!

61. Spiritual memory loss

...he is short-sighted and blind, and has forgotten that he has been cleansed from his past sins *(2 Peter 1:9).*

Spiritual memory loss happens to individuals – when they lose connection with their Christian past. In doing so, they lose their way through life.

You bump into them one Saturday morning, shopping in Selfridges.

'Hullo, Andy, Long time no see!'

'Oh, er – hullo. Yes, wait a minute; um ... Jeremy, isn't it?'

'That's me! Remember when we first met, sharing that student tent at the July Convention? And the decision we made together when we went forward? And those great Bible studies we heard on Ephesians?'

'Sorry, what was that? ... Oh, yeah, well ... that was a while back. Since then, I've sort of, well ... See you, then!'

He's forgotten. It's the difference between building your faith up steadily (see 2 Peter 1:5-8), and letting those earlier ties slacken imperceptibly. Let it go on like that, and you can lose connection altogether with the very things that give you a basis for life and the future (Colossians 2:19).

Have you forgotten?

62. He comes triumphant!

Rejoice, rejoice you people of Zion! Shout for joy, people of Jerusalem! Look, your king is coming to you! He comes triumphant and victorious, but humble and riding on a donkey – on a colt, the foal of a donkey *(Zechariah 9:9 GNB).*

'We're pulling into the side!' Our African driver swung the car onto the rough verge. Blazing headlights were coming towards us and sirens were blaring. Then a phalanx of motorbike outriders; next, armoured cars, followed by a military truck crammed with rocket launchers. In the middle of the convoy was a Mercedes. Seconds later the entire cavalcade was a receding speck on the dusty horizon. *The President had just gone by....*

Yes, in that part of Africa, the leadership was on a knife-edge of insecurity. But the world longs for a different kind of rule. It was in one of the darkest hours of the Jewish nation that a prophecy of hope was once given by Zechariah, the prophet of restoration.

Amazingly it was fulfilled to the letter six centuries later, as Jesus rode into Jerusalem – not with a flourish of power, but as a Servant King on a donkey. He looks a loser rather than a winner. But His rule would be a billion times more effective for the world than any speeding convoy of rocket launchers.

The world longs for a different kind of rule.

63. Eternal life?

If a man dies, will he live again? *(Job 14:14).*

Of all the questions ever framed, whether by stone-age people, tribal people, industrial, digital or IT people, this is the most universal.

1. Look at the question speculatively
Whether it was the mummified processing of Egyptian funeral rites, the Elysian fields of the Greek philosophers, or the Scandinavian hopes of *Valhalla*, there has always been a wistfulness about a possible after-death *existence* – little more than that. Nobody really knew a thing.

2. Look at the question historically
A man *did* die; died in full, public view. The man whose tomb he was buried in was known by name, and a guard was set. Yet, on the third day the tomb was empty – except for the graveclothes still twirled, shell-like, around a body that was no longer there. There were many witnesses – *and the story held, despite death threats.* Only one life has ever done it.

3. Look at the question personally
If *I* die, will *I* live again? The Christ of the resurrection declares, 'He who believes in me will live, even though he dies' (John 11:25). Knowing Christ is the ultimate – in fact the *only* – secret of living eternally. Would you like that? Come on in! *Start today.*

Knowing Christ is the *only* secret of living eternally.

64. Are you saved?

Believe on the Lord Jesus Christ, and thou shalt be saved *(Acts 16:31).*

On Sunday, April 14th, 1912, the *Titanic* went down in the Atlantic on her maiden voyage. Some years later, at a meeting in Hamilton, Canada, a young Scotsman stood up to speak:

'I was on the Titanic, when she sank. Drifting alone on a spar in the icy water in that awful night, a wave brought John Harper of Glasgow near to me. He too was holding onto a piece of wreck. "Man, are you saved?" he shouted. "No, I am not", was my reply. He answered, "Believe on the Lord Jesus Christ, and thou shalt be saved".

'The waves bore him away, but a little later he was washed back alongside me. "Are you saved now?" he said. "No", I replied, "I cannot honestly say that I am". Once more he repeated the verse, "Believe on the Lord Jesus Christ, and thou shalt be saved".

'Then, losing his hold, he sank. And there, alone in the night, and with two miles of water under me, I *believed*. I am John Harper's last convert'.

Visit, one day, the John Harper Memorial Church in Glasgow, or the similar memorial at the Moody Church in Chicago. And get inspired!

It's never too late to witness – or to believe.

65. Remember with gratitude

I thank my God every time I remember you *(Philippians 1:3).*

Yes, there are those who, when people think of them, arouse feelings of gratitude – even inspiration. I was one of some million people who stood once in London's streets to see Queen Elizabeth the Queen Mother's coffin go by – for I remember her with thanksgiving. She was able to inspire millions.

I was only four when I first saw her – riding with the King in a horse-drawn carriage out of Buckingham Palace. My missionary parents – on leave from Kenya – had asked that my two brothers and I should be allowed inside the Palace gates, to see the royal couple ride out. **We were allowed in**. We dressed suitably in sailor suits – learning that the King would be in naval uniform. We rehearsed our saluting technique.

The moment arrived. Out came the carriage – and we saluted. The Queen spotted us first. She nudged the King and pointed to us. Immediately the King stood up – in the moving carriage – *and saluted us back*. Later my older brother wrote a letter of thanks. 'Darling Queen ...' it began.

One incident. There were thousands of stories like this. A tiny incident has the capacity to inspire – and to be remembered for ever.

Who do you remember with gratitude?

66. Hidden treasure

But we have this treasure in jars of clay, to show that this all-surpassing power is from God and not from us *(2 Corinthians 4:7).*

That famous Koh-i-Noor diamond, featuring on the crown of Britain's former Queen Mother – why, it was a glowing illustration of the bright jewel of Christ's Gospel, shining across the highroads of time.

Where shall we display this blazing stone? *Maybe we can find an old jam jar under the stairs?* 'Jars of clay', earthen flower pots? That'll do nicely!

This is the style of God's kingdom. When the Son of God was born on earth, what site was found for his unique birth? That cowshed over there; let's start with that. And that animals' eating trough ... er, we can always clean it up a bit. That artisan home of a Jewish joiner – why not? That bunch from the Israeli fishing industry – they might make tolerable representatives for the new movement.

It has been like this all the way along. The all-surpassing **power** is not found in that beautiful cathedral, or that brilliant music. As for that speaker with the gift of oratory – apart from God's power, he's no more than a piece of putty. We must give credit where credit is due. The power to change lives and society resides in God and the Gospel of Christ. Nowhere else.

**The power to change lives and society
resides in God and the Gospel of Christ.**

67. Small radical beginnings

Teach slaves to be subject to their masters ... so that ... they will make the teaching about God our Saviour attractive *(Titus 2:9, 10)*.

The Christian slaves of the Roman empire, says the apostle Paul, were to be submissive, honest and faithful.

A little tame for a sensational new religion? Might we have looked for something more radical; a call for revolt, a revolution? But that would have been to reduce Christ to the level of a mere Spartacus or Karl Marx.

No, Christians were to be more revolutionary still. Within their own fellowship they simply chose to treat the demarcations between slaves and masters *as though they didn't exist at all* (Galatians 3:28). Such distinctions simply became irrelevant. The New Testament letter to Philemon (himself a slave owner) said it all. He was to treat Onesimus, his returned runaway slave, '**no longer as a slave, but as a dear brother**' (Philemon 16).

'What an attractive faith' people might say, as they looked at the consistent lives of those slaves. Yes – but powerful too. There it was, ticking like a time bomb in the heart of the Roman empire, until one day the church would stand over its grave. And the day would come when slavery would be officially outlawed....

In what way is your faith revolutionary today?

68. Christ's Ascension

The time approached for him to be taken up to heaven *(Luke 9:51)*.

At this ninth chapter of Luke, the half-way mark of the Gospel story has been reached. The ultimate goal is beginning to come into sight – *and it is perceived as being the bodily ascension of Jesus*. Reason – the ascension would be the final divine crowning of Jesus as universal Saviour.

Christ had come on a mission of salvation to the world. **The birth at Bethlehem inaugurated it. The baptism at Jordan announced it. The Cross of Calvary achieved it. The resurrection at Easter endorsed it. And now the Ascension celebrated it. The Spirit at Pentecost then drove it, world-wide!**

Luke makes mention of Christ's being 'taken up into heaven' again, at the end of his Gospel (Luke 24:51). And again, when he writes of it in Acts 1: 2 and 9. The attendant angels then tell the disciples, 'This same Jesus, *who has been taken from you into heaven*, will come back in the same way you have seen him go into heaven' (Acts 1:11).

In an inter-religious debate I was challenged as to whether there was a single statement in the Bible that Christ had been taken up to heaven. These are some of the verses. Why not memorise them?

This same Jesus will come back.

69. Spirit-filled Christians

Do not get drunk on wine, which leads to debauchery. Instead, be filled with the Spirit *(Ephesians 5:18).*

Two contrasting kinds of intoxication – and the better way is to be filled, *controlled,* by the Spirit of the Lord Jesus Christ. A few surprises ...

1. Spirit-filled people are more aware of Christ than they are of the Spirit.

There is this strange anonymity about the Holy Spirit. He comes into the life of every believer – not to draw attention to Himself, but to Jesus (John 16:14). A Spirit-filled *church*, then, is always Christ-centred.

2. Spirit-filled people are more concerned with 'emptying' than with 'filling'.

We are not to hug our blessings to ourselves, but to share them with others. Don't you feel better at the *end* of a piece of service for the Lord, than at the beginning? The way to be filled is to be emptied!

3. Spirit-filled people are more concerned for the interests of others than for their own.

This was true of people like Stephen the martyr. It was observed by *others* that he was filled with the Spirit; he made no such public claim for himself. Of course not – he was always thinking of others.

The way to be filled is to be emptied!

70. Sons and daughters

For you did not receive a spirit that makes you a slave again to fear, but you have received the Spirit of sonship *(Romans 8:15).*

Sons, and daughters. How sensationally faith in Jesus Christ contrasts with every other belief-system going! In numerous religions, the deity – or deities – are a remote being, aloof, forbidding, distant, and to be feared.

The servant or slave does not know what his master is doing, said Jesus (John 15:15). But how different is the situation when we are in the family. Within it, confidences are shared – *and there is always access.*

When our children were little, sometimes our bedroom door would crash open in the early hours of the morning ... and a little pyjama-clad figure would hurtle across the room and jump into bed between us – as often as not clutching a toy tractor. They had access to us. Of course. *They were family.* It wasn't just anybody we would allow to come into bed with us!

It is to Jesus, supremely, that we owe this concept of a loving Father to whom we have immediate and intimate access through Christ.

Are you in the family yet? The way in is through Jesus Christ. When we receive His Spirit into our lives, we receive the Spirit who makes us sons and daughters.

Are you in the family yet?

71. Times of challenge

I will stand at my watch and station myself on the ramparts; I will look to see what He will say to me, and what answer I am able to give to this complaint *(Habakkuk 2:1).*

There were troops massing on the border. Insecurity on every side. The Battle of Carchemish had taken place in 605 BC, and nothing seemed stable any more.

Yet the prophet Habakkuk found strength in staying at his post – and in so doing was able to inspire others. For us, too, to *'stand at your watch'* is to be at the place of vigilance – and prayerful intercession.

1. We watch in a position of stability.
'The ramparts' implies this. Prayer and intercession *always* build a platform of strength.

2. We watch in a position of serenity.
'I will look to see what *He* will say to me'. Habakkuk knew that human-based solutions would collapse. It is with confidence, then, that we too may spread the situation before God.

3. We watch in a position of authority.
From the vantage point of prayer and waiting on God, we can expect an 'answer'.

> **At times of challenge, what the church is**
> **doing is of more importance to the world**
> **than the actions of any other group.**

72. Revival

O Lord, revive thy work in the midst of the years. ... in wrath, remember mercy *(Habakkuk 3:2 KJV).*

God's people, like those in the time of Habakkuk the prophet, have always wistfully longed for a mighty revival to break out in times of insecurity and spiritual dryness. But how and when does a revival occur?

Ultimately it is an action of the sovereign God. The Spirit moves like the blowing of an unpredictable wind (John 3:8). *We* cannot bring about a spiritual revival. Yet we can learn and be prepared from Christian history – so that when God moves, we move with Him! I grew up in the East African Revival. Four great characteristics accompany such a revival:

1. Widespread moral repentance at the preaching of the blood of Christ.
This leads to a noticeable upgrading of behaviour.

2. Hundreds of thousands of conversions to Jesus Christ.
Even whole villages can convert *en masse*, when God's Spirit is on the move.

3. Mighty preaching from the Bible.
The appetite for the *Bible* will spread like a bush fire.

4. Deep-seated intercessory prayer
– for neighbours, relations, work-colleagues, for a dying world.

Lord God, in the midst of these years,
begin a revival, and begin it in me

Begin a revival, and begin it in me

73. Strength in God

The sovereign Lord is my strength; he makes my feet like the feet of a deer; he enables me to go to the heights *(Habakkuk 3:19).*

That last sentence of Habakkuk's prophecy is a far cry from his first utterance: 'How long, O Lord, must I call for help, but you do not listen?'(Habakkuk 1:2). Here is a remarkable transference from the pit of desolation to walking on air! It was not done by mental sleight of hand or wishful thinking. The dangers from the hostile oppressor, Babylon, were real enough, and so were the questions raised:

Is God **paralysed**? (Chapter 1:1-11) ... Is God **good**? (1:12–2:1) ... Is God **late**? (2:2-5) ... Will God **win**? (2:6-20).

But all the way along, the prophet held on like a limpet to the granite conviction that his God was the God who marches through history, overturning one nation, and then another – if necessary, even allowing His own people to be exiled in shame, to bring them to their senses.

Habakkuk had his doubts – but it was always doubt within commitment. Notice the ascending order of his resolves: '**I will stand and look**' (2:1); '**I will wait**' (3:16); '**I will rejoice**' (3:18). Although the Babylonians were at the gate, his trust in God was secure. *Nothing else mattered.*

His trust in God was secure. *Nothing else mattered.*

74. Resurrection hope

Lord, if you had been here, my brother would not have died
(John 11:32).

Mary was weeping. Her brother Lazarus had died four days earlier and Jesus had come, well, a little too late. Jesus wept too. Yet the account of the raising of Lazarus is shot through with His authority. Three phrases:

1. The power to remove: 'Take away the stone' (v. 39). The gravestone symbolised the crushing weight of dread that had always clung around death. This, then, was to be the removal of more than a stone – but of *ignorance, and despair*. We would never think in the same way again.

2. The power to reverse: 'Lazarus, come out!' (v. 43). Another command. This was epoch-making – four long days after the funeral!

3. The power to release: 'Unbind him, and let him go' (v. 44). 'Go'? Go where? Why back to the old home in Bethany. It would be lunch time in a few minutes. It was Lazarus' turn to do the washing up! Next, the tax returns. He was *back* into the old life. One day he would die again.

Yes, this was only the curtain-raiser to **the big event** – the resurrection of Jesus – which assures his followers not of a going back, but a going on, to an eternal, resurrection body. Do you have a stake in this?

Do you have a stake in Jesus' resurrection?

75. The truth will set you free

Then you will know the truth, and the truth will set you free'
(John 8:32).

Truth can surface in the strangest places. It was the old Soviet leader, Mr Andropov, who would declare, 'There is an old Russian saying ...' and then proceed to quote Scripture! Here now are Jesus' words in John's Gospel – to challenge the world.

Truth as a passion. Some modern thinkers are fond of talking about *truths* rather than Truth – but there is in the heart, everywhere, a basic desire to know the Ultimate – about ourselves, our universe, origin and destiny (Ecclesiastes 3:11).

Truth as a power. In the end, it is never the military people, nor the politicians who have dictated the course of history – but the *ideas* people. Truth cannot be held down for ever. There is nothing better than at last *understanding*. Jesus does that, even for illiterates.

Truth as a Person. Jesus' hearers that day resented his statement, 'If the Son sets you free, you will be free indeed' (v. 36). The clue to understanding – and true liberation – lies in Him. It is not that He simply speaks the truth. All truth – scientific, philosophical and moral holds together and centres in Him.

**If you abandon Jesus as Truth's centre,
you become *eccentric*.**

76. Greater things

Anyone who has faith in me will do what I have been doing. He will do even greater things than these, because I am going to the Father *(John 14:12)*.

Whatever did Jesus mean by this saying? No one – no one at all – has ever out-performed Him in the field of miracles, either in quality or quantity. That only needs ten seconds thought! Who else in history could still storms at a word, heal leprosy sufferers at a touch, feed 5,000 from virtually nothing, walk on water or raise someone after four days in the grave?

Greater things? The key to understanding this sentence lies in the words, 'because I am going to the Father'. As Christ's bodily presence was withdrawn from the world, so His Spirit was sent, to accomplish – through the ministry of ordinary believers – 'greater things', *not of a superior physical kind, but of a superior dimension altogether.* The conversion of the 3,000 at Pentecost was a 'greater thing' than the feeding of the 5,000 by Lake Galilee. Every time someone is born again, and becomes a follower of Jesus – in China, India or Australia, it is a 'greater thing'.

**See if you can put John 14:12 into
practice during this very week.**

77. Discipleship

So therefore, any one of you who does not renounce all that he has cannot be my disciple *(Luke 14:33 RSV).*

So, where's the attraction? The prospective disciple faces stern tests!

1. The love test. Verse 26 tells us that, by comparison to love of Christ, disciples are to 'hate' their families. This is the typical Semitic terminology of **selection** ('Jacob I loved, but Esau I hated' – *Romans 9:13*). All earthly loves – while they can indeed be enhanced by the overriding love of Christ – must nevertheless come second to it.

2. The death test. *Bearing the cross* is the next test (v. 27). It means putting your own interests second – even to the point of death. We are not here for a boating trip!

3. The finishing test. Two parables follow (vv. 28-32); one, a man who failed to count the cost of his building project, the other about a monarch weighing up the issues before embarking on a costly war. No disciple wants to be consigned to history's book of heroic failures.

Is Christian discipleship worth it? The attraction lies in the magnetic pull exerted by the Man of Galilee himself. We hear his voice; we glimpse his person – and something inside says, '**I will follow this Man to the ends of the earth.**'

Is Christian discipleship worth it?

78. To the ends of the earth

You will be my witnesses ... to the ends of the earth *(Acts 1:8)*.

We were having a family holiday picnic on a grassy hillside, just outside Mombasa, on the East African coast. Suddenly one of us tripped on something hard in the undergrowth. It turned out to be a gravestone – completely overgrown.

Peering closer – and seeing the famous name *Krapf* inscribed on the stone – the dramatic nature of our discovery overwhelmed us. Dr Ludwig Krapf of Germany had been sent out as the Church Missionary Society's first pioneer to East Africa in 1844. Almost on arrival at Mombasa, malaria struck down his wife and baby girl; they were buried in what was described as 'a lonely missionary grave' ... and Ludwig pressed on into the interior.

It was with emotion and thanksgiving that we spent the rest of the afternoon tidying up the grave.

It happened to Krapf, and it is going to go on happening until the end of time. Christ fills His people with power, and then sends them out to take His good news to others. So great is the power of His call that, if it comes to it, they will leave their bones in the places that he sends them to.

Christ fills His people with power, and then sends them out to take His good news to others.

79. Giving

I tell you the truth, this poor widow has put more money into the treasury than all the others *(Mark 12:43).*

Motives differ when it comes to giving. Some give on *the tip level*, some on *the habit level*, others on the *impulse level*, and just a few on the *ostentatious level*, like the show-offs that Jesus here exposes (v. 40).

Christ measures devotion not by our words, but by our deeds

For 'measuring' is what He does, as the crowds pass by the temple treasury. The widow's two coins represent the umpteen jam-jars, missionary boxes and furtively-scrawled envelopes of 2,000 years!

Christ measures devotion not by our gifts but by our hearts

It is the motivation that is vital. Giving, at its best, is deliberate, calculating and proportional. 'On the first day of every week, each of you is to put something aside and store it up, as he may prosper' (1 Corinthians 16:2).

Christ measures devotion not by what we give but by what we keep

The widow could have given only one of her two copper coins. Even then it would have represented 50% of her resources. As it was, the temple – a corrupt religious institution – got the lot. No strings attached to this donor's giving! She had out-thought and out-given every donor in sight.

> **Christ measures devotion not by what we give but by what we keep.**

80. Real wealth

The Christian who is poor must be glad when God lifts him up, and the rich Christian must be glad when God brings him down. For the rich will pass away like the flower of a wild plant *(James 1:9, 10 GNB).*

Wherever the American dollar sign is printed, there is a reminder of the famous pillars of Hercules at the straits of Gibralter. On old Spanish coins the two great Rocks were represented by twin vertical pillars, and a garland was twined about them. Those coins were the ancestors of the American dollar ... thus even the dollar binds us to our past. So the thread of human history runs through the world of our modern money. It has always been tied into every day of life. *But it is not life itself.*

'Wealth is like a viper', said Clement of Alexandria. Money is a useful tool, but to many people it is a crushing tyrant. Its main danger lies in its power to delude us, to sidetrack us from the actual adventure and creativity of living upon, this, the only inhabited planet in the universe. Once let God – and the life-giving words of Jesus Christ – colour our thinking, and we can begin to live at last, no longer robbed by the world's obsession with money.

**Let God colour your thinking,
and you can begin to live at last.**

81. Pride

For by the grace given me I say to every one of you: Do not think of yourself more highly than you ought... *(Romans 12:3).*

It is unfortunate that most of our friends will never tell us if we are behaving and speaking in a conceited, self-centred way. We have to rely upon the preaching we hear, the Bible we read – and supremely upon the Christ we follow – if we are to take ourselves in hand on this very personal issue.

Where are all the arrows of attention pointing? Leaving aside ourselves (which we must never do), it is the easiest thing in the world to spot the arrogant strutters of this world, whether in politics, at the workplace, within the family or at church. Every conversation, every gesture and action is somehow manipulated to draw attention to themselves and their achievements. All the arrows are pointing inwards – never outwards to others. They become noted for it – but they are almost certainly unaware of the reputation that is theirs.

Is this you? Do a little rough and ready assessment of yourself over these next ten minutes. Where are the arrows pointing? Be sure of this, if they are directed perpetually at yourself, **no one will ever tell you.**

Where are the arrows pointing in your life?

82. God's touch

With the tip of his staff that was in his hand, the angel of the Lord touched the meat and the unleavened bread. Fire flared from the rock, consuming the meat and the bread *(Judges 6:21).*

It only takes a single generation for everyone to forget. To listen to the media today, you would think that the Reformation never took place 400 years ago in Britain, that John Wesley had never preached those 40,000 sermons that transformed the life of England. And back in the twelfth and eleventh centuries BC, the weak and leaderless people of Israel had forgotten about God's rescue of them from Egypt; it was as though Moses had never lived. Nothing now seemed powerful enough to lift their morale.

But it only takes a single touch from God and the scene can change. Gideon gives his heavenly visitor a meal. One touch of a staff on the meat course was enough to convince the farmer that God's power was on him as Israel's new leader.

The great mission pioneer Hudson Taylor said, a hundred years ago, 'God chose me because I was weak enough. God does not do his great works by large committees. He trains somebody to be quiet enough and little enough, and then he uses *him.*'

**'God chose me because I was
weak enough'. Hudson Taylor**

83. Involved in Christ's Mission

Jesus said to Philip, 'How are we to buy bread, so that these people may eat?' This he said to test him, for he himself knew what he would do *(John 6:5, 6).*

At the height of the preparations for a Billy Graham mission in London, I was chairing a committee meeting. How difficult everything seemed! At one point I turned to Norman Sanders, a Graham team member.

'Norman', I said, 'With all your experience of these missions, give us some advice. How shall we solve this impasse?'

Norman replied, 'Let's take encouragement from John 6 – where it looked impossible, but where we also read that Jesus himself *knew what he would do.* He's in charge, not us!'

It's the key reminder for all difficulties facing Christ's workers. For Philip, the feeding of 5,000 people looked impossible. But Jesus was there, and this made the difference.

Why – if it all depended upon Jesus – did He bother to consult Philip at all? The reason is that the Lord has chosen for us to be **involved** in His mission to this world. He also allows us to be **tested**, in the stretching of our trust. And then, seeing His power at work means that we shall also be **inspired** – for future occasions. There's always a 'next time'!

The Lord has chosen for us to be
involved **in His mission to this world.**

84. Strength in weakness

But he said to me, 'My grace is sufficient for you, for my power is made perfect in weakness' *(2 Corinthians 12:9).*

Have you ever heard of Fanny Crosby? She was a fine nineteenth century illustration of this principle dominating the two letters to the Corinthians.

Afflicted by an eye infection when only a baby, she was given the wrong treatment by a doctor, who placed hot poultices on her eyes. When the bandages were taken off, Fanny could see nothing beyond an impression of frosted glass.

But her Puritan background and her godly grandmother meant that Fanny grew up 'seeing' all of life by the power of her imagination. She learnt Scripture. By the time she was ten she had memorised all first five books of the Bible, together with the four Gospels, the whole of the Psalms, and plenty more. The rich theology in her soul she then poured into hymn writing. **Blessed Assurance, To God be the Glory, He hideth my soul in the cleft of the Rock**. All in all she wrote 9,000 hymns that have fed Christians and influenced the spirituality of churches worldwide. *The Bible was her fuel, the cross was her centre – and the heart was her target!* Try her hymns, and you'll find out.

The Bible was her fuel, the cross was her centre – and the heart was her target!

85. Disciple of Christ

The Lord commanded us to obey all these decrees and to fear the Lord our God, so that we might always prosper and be kept alive , as is the case today *(Deuteronomy 6:24).*

'If we are not governed by God,' said William Penn, 'then we will be governed by tyrants.' That was back in 1681.

The 'Freedom!' cry of the 1960s was followed by a new authoritarianism from around the 1980s. On the religious front, groups and sectarian-like churches became dominated by one charismatic leader at the top, with members disciplined rigidly at every level.

Of course, to some it is not an unattractive way to live. There is a certain 'security' about signing over your house, your money and your will to a central authority. True, you're a slave – but you have a roof over your head and someone else is making all your decisions for you!

For the biblical Christian (and that's the only kind of Christian there can be), the whole edifice falls to pieces with the simple realisation, *I am a disciple of one Man only.* When God in Christ is seen as the final arbiter for all of life, we enter as 'slaves' under the authority of a leader whom to serve is, strangely, perfect freedom.

Am I a disciple of one man only?

86. Christ's return

In the year that King Uzziah died I saw the Lord sitting upon a throne, high and lifted up; and his train filled the temple *(Isaiah 6:1).*

Have you realised that Isaiah – when he declared the vision that he had seen – **'said this because he saw Jesus' glory and spoke about him'** (John 12:41)?

Jesus does not begin half way through history! He has repeatedly manifested Himself in brilliant glory, both before and after His incarnation as man. He did so here in Isaiah 6, in Daniel 7:13-14 and in Ezekiel 1:26-28. He is similarly irradiated in the New Testament account of the Transfiguration (Luke 9:28-36), at the martydom of Stephen (Acts 7:55-56) and on John's exile island of Patmos (Revelation 1:12-18).

Jesus has warned us ahead of time that at the end of the age He will return once more in overwhelming glory (Matthew 24:27-31). I have heard of some who acknowledge this – but fatuously claim that, on coming back, He will deny the cross! We have only to read Revelation 1:17, 18 to recognise this as an empty claim. No; whether on that final day He comes as our Saviour or as our Judge, depends upon what we did about the cross where He died for us. The time to get ready is now, *now*, **NOW**.

The time to get ready is now.

87. Called, chosen and faithful

With him will be his called, chosen and faithful followers
(Revelation 17:14).

Here is a passage to encourage followers of Jesus, world-wide and across all of time! John's vision in the book of Revelation tells the reader that the powers of evil will give their authority to 'the beast' (the embodiment of all that opposes Christ) – with the 'one purpose' of *making war against the Lamb* (vv. 12-14). Do you feel this opposition, Christian reader – along all fronts? I do.

Our encouragement derives, first, from the fact that these evil powers receive their authority for 'one hour' only (v. 12). They are not for ever! Secondly, 'the Lamb will overcome them' (v. 14). And thirdly, he will be accompanied by 'those who are with him', **called, chosen and faithful**.

People often wonder, 'How can I *know* if I'm one of the elect?'

Easy. Look up Isaiah 42:1, and you'll see that *Christ*, the coming Servant of the Lord is 'my chosen one in whom I delight'. He is the chosen one. It says so again in 1 Peter 2:4. And do you belong to Christ? Is your trust in Him? Are you 'with Him'? If so, then, **with Him**, you are chosen as well. It says so!

> **Are you 'with Him'? If so, then, *with Him*, you are chosen as well.**

88. Don't add to Scripture

Learn from us the meaning of the saying, 'Do not go beyond what is written' *(1 Corinthians 4:6).*

Here were Paul and Apollos, faced by counterfeit 'apostles'; men who sat loosely on the Scriptures, trusting much more in their natural gifts and personalities, and with an insatiable appetite for sensations, rather than for transformation of character. They'd left the Scriptures behind, long ago.

Preachers! Speakers! Bible group leaders! What do you rely on **most** in the sessions you are responsible for? In many circles a sermon or Bible study is not regarded as successful unless it features a stream of the latest funny stories. Let's just remember that about no great preacher of the world was it ever said, 'He was a terribly funny man.' No one ever came in repentance to the Cross of Calvary, laughing all the way.

Of course we can be story-tellers. Jesus was one such. And there's a place for humour. But the power doesn't lie in the anecdote; it really doesn't. Rather, let's see to it that it's the carefully applied message of the Bible that is central. And the attitude? Paul has it for us in 2 Corinthians 5:11, AV): **'Knowing therefore the terror of the Lord, we persuade men.'**

Shall we remember that, the very next time?

> **Let's see to it that it's the carefully**
> **applied message of the Bible that is central.**

89. Wars

From whence come wars and fightings among you? *(James 4:1 KJV).*

It's a scandal – the only inhabited planet in the universe and the wars among us indicate that *we cannot get on with each other.* Why is this?

1. The many projections. James tells us here that the outward disorders are only projections of the sinful heart. They 'come from your desires that battle within you' (v. 1). The *macro* sins on the big scale come out of the *micro* sins of fightings, backbitings and petty jealousies that can turn a small church into a civil war!

2. The two ways. The theme here condenses into an issue of two ways to live – and two only. It begins with the two kinds of *wisdom* (James 3:13-17), the 'unspiritual' and the 'heavenly'. If we 'choose' (4:4) the latter, the result will be peace-loving, considerate people, recognised as 'peacemakers' (3:18). *What is your own reputation in the church?*

3. The single authority. If, says James (4:11,12), you 'judge' your fellow Christian, it means that you have placed *yourself* in the seat of judgment. But there is only one Judge. Describe your own character! Go further and apply the active words of this passage to put yourself right – *choose* (4) *... submit ... resist* (7) *... Come ... wash ... purify* (8) *... Grieve ... Change* (9) *... Humble yourselves* (10).

A better world starts with you.

90. Who will stand in the gap?

And I sought for a man among them who should build up the wall and stand in the breach before me for the land, that I should not destroy it, but I found none *(Ezekiel 22:30 ESV).*

It sounds like a go-between man – or woman – that the Lord God was looking for, back in the days of Jewish exile. Who would be the one who would build up a wall of protection and help close the aperture; to stand in the gap – *through which would otherwise pour God's judgment?*

In every age, a body of faithful believers is called for, to witness, pray and preach on behalf of people in spiritual danger – so that the message of the cross of Jesus Christ may come to them and protect them from final destruction.

*Anyone can do it....*and the message surely is, **Be that person who will stand in the breach!** What kind of a person? Talented? No. Witty and oratorical? No. An organisational tyro? No. Rather, someone of **passion** (think of Abraham in Genesis 18, standing in the gap on behalf of Sodom and Gomorrah); someone of **prayer** (facing the world on behalf of God, and facing God on behalf of the world), and someone of **proclamation** – who can warn and woo! God says, 'I'm looking ... I'm looking – just for *SOMEONE.*'

Be that person who will stand in the breach!

91. How do we respond to failure?

And Peter went outside and wept bitterly.... Then [Judas] went away and hanged himself *(Matthew 26:75; 27:5).*

Here are two men who, on being exposed as failures, *departed*. But one is restored and the other self-destructs. Why? The clues lie in these areas:

1. Accountability. Put simply, it's the difference between the team *player* and the *loner*. Peter was always part of the team, sharing a particular chemistry with James and John. Judas however was always sloping off on his own – how was he spending his time? No one really knew. Servants of Christ needs a group to whom they are accountable.

2. Motivation. Here's the difference between being a lover of Christ and a lover of money. Of *course* Peter loved Jesus; for such there will always be a way back. But Judas was the materialist of the Bible, calculating and secretive (Matthew 26:15). Message: you can't serve God *and* money.

3. Memory. 'Then Peter *remembered*' (Matthew 26:75). He would never forget Christ's warning, nor the look on His face after the denial (Luke 22:61). Memory! It can offer us life – and a way back. But Judas really only had *money* for his memories ; so his remorse takes him in the wrong direction – to Christ's enemies. **Where do *we* fit into this cameo?**

Where do *we* fit into this cameo?

92. Christ's second Coming

...We wait for the blessed hope – the glorious appearing of our great God and Saviour, Jesus Christ *(Titus 2:13).*

Here is a clear affirmation of Christ as God. True, the literal Greek *could* mean 'the appearing of our great God (the Father), and our Saviour Jesus Christ' – but nowhere in the New Testament is God (the Father) said to 'appear'. Every one of the ten 'appearing' references are of Jesus. And this is how the Greek church leaders of early Christian history understood the passage – and I guess that their Greek was better than ours!

Actually the reference *has* to be to Christ, because the sentence runs on to describe his sacrificial death (v. 14).

So, Christ, our Saviour and our God, will 'appear' at the end of the age. He came first, in the 'grace of God' (v. 11), at Bethlehem. That coming was humble, localised – and witnessed only by a few. The second Coming will be different. It will be 'glorious' and it will be universal. *You will be there, whether or not you wish it.* And whether or not you wish it, you will bow to His authority – either joyfully as one of 'his very own' (v. 14) or in crushing judgement that will consign you to outer darkness. The day of choosing – and of 'grace' (v. 11) is **now**.

The day of choosing is *now*.

93. Everlasting Father

'Everlasting Father....' *(Isaiah 9:6).*

It's remarkable that this is one of the prophet Isaiah's four titles that described the 'child' ruler who was to be born. But some have asked, Are we in danger of confusing the divine Persons of the Trinity, by applying this name to Jesus Christ? Some of our critics even scoff that such a title – if it applies to Jesus – makes nonsense of Trinitarian teaching.

In my book *The Top 100 Questions* (Christian Focus Publications) this features as a 'difficult Bible passage' that requires an explanation. *Actually the answer is very close at hand, right in the immediate context.*

For in only the previous chapter this sentence occurs: **'Here am I, and the children the Lord has given me'** (Isaiah 8:18). Who is the speaker? Why, Hebrews 2:13 confirms that it's Christ! There it quotes the Isaiah verse, attributing it to Jesus, *'And again he says, "Here am I and the children God has given me."'*

It makes complete sense. We say of an evangelist who has led us to faith that he is our 'spiritual father.' This is *eternally* true of Christ, who – by His saving death – has produced millions upon millions of believers, 'children' of whom He is **Everlasting Father**. Are you one of them?

Are you one of His children?

94. The dragon and the Church

The dragon stood in front of the woman who was about to give birth, so that he might devour her child the moment it was born *(Revelation 12:4).*

The dragon? This passage of Revelation tells us that this is the devil, 'that ancient serpent' (v. 9). *The child?* That's easy; it's Jesus, 'a male child, who will rule all the nations with an iron sceptre' (v. 5). *The woman?* No, it's not Mary, it's **the Church**, the people of God. The clue lies in her description in verse 1 – 'clothed with the sun, with the moon under her feet and a crown of twelve stars on her head' – a reference to Joseph's dream in Genesis 37:9 where the children of Israel are portrayed by these symbols.

The birth pangs, mentioned in verse 2, were the numerous trials of history that preceded Jesus' historical coming to earth.

The message is that, from day one of God's loving plan to reclaim the wayward human race, every attempt imaginable was made to thwart the rescue bid and – if possible – to rub out the child and the woman (the Church) from which He was produced!

The powers of hell are bent on a hopeless quest. They try hard enough! But no one can stop Jesus. And His church will finally be standing over the smoking grave of the kingdom of evil.

His church will finally be standing over the smoking grave of the kingdom of evil.

95. God sent His Son

But when the time had fully come, God sent his Son, born of a woman *(Galatians 4:4).*

'But what a funny thing to say' – I hear the comment – *'born of a woman;* surely all human beings are going to begin their stay on the planet in that way!'

Yet that is the whole point about Christ's birth. God in person came to earth. Not in a touch-down landing, not for a brief inspection, not as an astronaut, phantom or detached seraph-like *guru,* but as a little boy, unable to speak a single word – even though the title of Bethlehem's baby was **The Word of God**!

The timing had all been worked out – the brilliant communications system of the **Roman** empire would eventually carry the message of Christ to all parts of Europe; the universal **Greek** language would save endless interpretation problems; the unfulfilled **Jewish** hopes and predictions of a Messiah provided the perfect cradle for what was about to happen. So there were no less than three civilisations co-operating to spread this message of the Son, born of a woman!

It's still spreading, friends. I can only speak for *evangelical* churches in Britain, of course. At one point membership in our churches increased by 68 % over a period of ten years. **Be part of the action yourself!**

Be part of the action yourself!

96. Fear not the future

For to me, to live is Christ and to die is gain *(Philippians 1:21).*

Christians, on reading the New Testament, learn that their life is from Christ....*in* Christ....*with* Christ....*for* Christ. But here is a sentence that covers the lot! How can we interpret this as a philosophy of life?

1. The Christ of every circumstance
Paul is writing this from prison. Some might have argued, 'Let me only be free from prison; *then* the Gospel can be preached.' But Paul's starting point is not himself but Christ. So many circumstances were against Paul but it is the Lord Jesus Christ who dominates his whole horizon – in which case, *nothing else matters.*

2. The Christ of life and death
The prisoner is hovering between life and death (vv. 22-24). But because Jesus is Lord of *both* these areas, Paul can't quite make up his mind which of the two is preferable. True, death is never less than an enemy – but under the rule and victory of Christ, it becomes a *gateway.*

3. The Christ of all the future
Paul is full of confidence for the unknown things that lie ahead for him (vv. 25, 26). The word 'joy' keeps surfacing in this remarkable prison letter. The Christian can echo words spoken once by American Gospel singer George Beverley Shea, **'Fear not tomorrow. God is already there!'**

Fear not tomorrow. God is already there!

97. The mystery of the Gospel

This mystery is that through the Gospel the Gentiles are heirs together with Israel, members together of one body and sharers together in the promise in Christ Jesus *(Ephesians 3:6).*

'Mystery' here is a truth, hidden in the past – at least partially – but now blown open. The key word here, occurring three times, is *together.*

These Ephesian Christians were now incorporated into a single body of believers, 'together' with all *Jewish* believers in Jesus. Gentiles today can come straight in by a side-gate into the age-old covenant, first made with Abraham ... just like that!

It's Jesus who has made this possible, by fulfilling in His saving death all the obligations of the Old Testament law – and He's done it both for Jews and Gentiles who now believe in Him. In the past it was apparent that God's salvation was for all – but now Christ's arrival has made it blazingly clear! This is why the wise men from the east were so full of joy, coming – as Gentiles – to worship the new-born Jesus.

Is there one system for Jews and another for Gentiles then? No! Christ 'has made the two **one**....*one new man* out of the two' (Ch. 2, vv. 14, 15). Jews, certainly, but also Koreans, Nigerians, Arabs, Americans, Danes and Brits! We have them all in a church I love: All Souls, Langham Place, London.

Christ has made the two one.

98. If the Lord is with us ...

Is the Lord among us or not? *(Exodus 17:7).*

A new prospect, a new job or a new year – everyone faces these things, and Moses was no exception. The miracle of the Red Sea crossing was over; now he and the vast company with him were out, into the novelty and unnerving experience of a completely new country. *'Is the Lord among us or not?'* You ask such a question when you find yourself:

1. Across the border.
Israel's wilderness adventures are a kind of model of the Christian life. Crossing the border is like being converted to Christ. The new situation can be frightening; yet if Christ is with you, nothing else matters!

2. In the wilderness.
The tendency is to grumble when adversity sets in – criticism from old friends, fighting old habits. It was Israel's problem too. It was when the going was hard, that they would question whether the Lord was with them. But remember, when you've crossed over, the **biggest** problem is *solved*.

3. Under attack.
The battles began and new Christians are aware that a whole bundle of problems *begin* at conversion! But it's a good sign; it's an indication that we really have changed sides. And if the Lord is with us nothing else matters!

If the Lord is with us....nothing else matters!

99. Sabbath

Which is lawful on the Sabbath; to do good or to do evil? *(Mark 3:4).*

Whether the Jewish Saturday or the Christian Sunday, the one-in-seven principle is stamped upon the world. And Jesus enhanced it.

1. Jesus has enhanced the Sabbath as creation day.
Naturally Jesus' critics had heard this before *but they'd forgotten it.* They had festooned it with rules and regulations. Jesus, through the Gospel, didn't create *another* day of rest; rather he renewed it as a day of Creation, or should we say *re*-Creation? In this way:

2. Jesus has enhanced the Sabbath as liberation day.
The religious leaders, he said, 'tie on to people's backs loads that are heavy and hard to carry' (Matthew 23:4). But Jesus, the greatest burden-bearer ever, *lifted* the one-in-seven day, freed it from its shackles, and made it a day of liberation – for workers and for those needing hospitality, love and service.

3. Jesus has enhanced the Sabbath as resurrection day.
It's not just Easter that is the day of witness to the Resurrection – it's every Sunday! Sunday steadily became the breaking of bread day (Acts 20:7), thank-offering day (1 Corinthians 16:2) and a challenge to one and all to stop and consider the universal claims of Christ. **Enjoy** your Sunday!

Enjoy **your Sunday!**

100. If the props are removed

Does Job fear God for naught? *(Job 1:9 KJV).*

Satan's jibe was that Job's faith would only persist while life looked good. But what if the props are removed? The book of Job puts these questions:

1. Does Job invite our confidence rather than our cynicism? The unbelieving world, like Satan, will always be cynical about believers who have life easy. Satan is out to get Job – but he's also out to get *God* – and over his best person. Let's see what happens when the roof falls in!

2. Will Job value character rather than wealth? It's the classic test. The Bible bristles with examples of believing people who crashed because of the lure of materialism – *Achan....Saul....Gehazi.... Judas....Demas.* Job is a universal figure for us all. How would we get on?

3. Can Job cope with the darkness as well as the light? Adversity strikes – and the hardest bit is '*Why?*' We readers know what's happening but the whole point is that Job is kept in the dark. *And he hangs on.* Only at the end he experiences God for himself, and then says, 'I had heard of Thee by the hearing of the ear, but now my eye *sees* Thee' (Job 42:5).

**The time to face these questions
is *now*; now, before life gets harder.**

101. What is man?

You made him ruler over the works of your hands; you put everything under his feet *(Psalm 8:6)*.

Psalm 8 is only a reflection of the mandate of Genesis to the human race, to act as custodians and overseers of the created order. Despite the grief and mourning that inevitably follow accidents in space, there is no stopping the human investigation of our amazing universe. The insatiable curiosity planted within our instincts is a God-given thing.

Years ago James Irwin, one of the crew in the moon-landing *Apollo 15*, spoke reverently of the wonders he had experienced back in 1969. And yet, coming to All Souls Church later on, during a visit to London, he drew attention to an even greater wonder. Presenting a framed and signed photograph of the event to the church, he wrote in his own hand an inscription below the picture. His words vividly sum up what Psalm 8 is telling us: **God walking on the earth is more important than man walking on the moon.**

The visited planet! Out of all the whirling constellations, we are the only planet that has been personally and historically visited by the Creator. Have you come to know Him yet, in His Son Jesus Christ?

God walking on the earth more important than man walking on the moon.

102. Jesus

I am the way, the truth and the life; no one comes to the Father, but by me *(John 14:6).*

Sometimes it is said that these words of Jesus may have been valid *for that time*, but that since then there have been fresh manifestations of God, further representatives who have superseded Christ. Let me give four reasons why this can never be:

1. God has spoken finally and uniquely by His Son. Although there is plenty more for us to *learn*, there is nothing more outside Jesus that God has to *say* to the human race. That being so, we are already living in the 'last days'. Look up Hebrews 1:1-3.

2. What Jesus did on the cross, he did for ever. He has died for our sins 'once for all', 'at the end of time' and 'for ever.' Have a look at Hebrews 9:26-28 and 1 Peter 1:18-21.

3. No one else has ever improved on Jesus. Morally, and in every way, he stands alone. There has never been another to match Him. See Hebrews 7:26 and 1 Peter 2:21-25.

4. Jesus warned us against future 'Christs'. 'Don't believe them!' Study Matthew 24:23-27. The *only* time Christ will reappear will be at the end of the age – suddenly, publicly, universally and finally.

> **The *only* time Christ will reappear**
> **will be at the end of the age.**

103. The sign of Jonah

A wicked and adulterous generation asks for a miraculous sign! But none will be given it except the sign of the prophet Jonah. For as Jonah was three days and three nights in the belly of a huge fish, so the Son of Man will be three days and three nights in the heart of the earth *(Matthew 12:39, 40).*

Jesus points his critics to one 'sign' only; his saving death – and subsequent Resurrection. This 'sign of the prophet Jonah' is big enough to meet our deepest needs for all time.

Some have argued that if Jesus was crucified on a Friday and only rose 'on the third day', then he was manifestly *not* in the grave for 'three days and three nights'. The Bible, they claim, is inaccurate.

But all that is unnecessary. In Jewish measuring, even a portion of a day (however small) was to be counted as a full 'day and a night'. Thus the Jewish Queen Esther could declare a period of fasting for three days and nights (Esther 4:16), when in fact she ended the fast '**on the third day**' (Esther 5:1). There is no problem.

The only problem occurs if we refuse to accept this vital 'sign' of Christ's sacrificial death, and neglect to act on it for our own salvation.

The problem occurs if we refuse to accept this vital 'sign' of Christ's sacrificial death.

104. Persecution

After his suffering, he showed himself to these men and gave many convincing proofs that he was alive *(Acts 1:3).*

The book of Acts is just about the most important book ever written, for it explains so much! It explains how a bunch of eleven demoralised Jews came to be the backbone of a movement that was eventually to replace the established Greek and heathen thought-forms that dominated all Europe, finally to become the biggest world belief-system of all.

Anyone who wants to discredit the recorded facts of the New Testament has got Luke to settle with, who – by painstaking research – established through eyewitness accounts the events that gave the church its launchng pad.

And cynics would also have martyrs to settle with – right up to the present day. When Pastor Paul Negrut first came over to the West from Communist Romania, he was confronted by a number of liberal doubting churchmen. They told him, 'No, no – you don't have to believe in the historical truth of all this!'

'No?' retorted Pastor Negrut. 'Don't you realise that we who suffered under Ceaucescu were willing to be tortured for these truths; I myself was! And some of us died for them.'

Read Acts at a sitting, and be convinced yourself.

105. Christ will return

Why do you stand here looking into the sky? This same Jesus, who has been taken from you into heaven, will come back in the same way you have seen him go into heaven *(Acts 1:11)*.

Every word of Acts chapter 1 is lit with significance. The apostles were gazing into the sky because their leader, Jesus, had been removed from their presence, bodily, visibly and publicly – and unmistakably away from their own familiar world. His saving work for reclaiming the human race was *done*.

But the angelic messengers then make plain to the eleven apostles that the very same person who had left them would be back – in the same way: bodily, visibly and publicly.

Can you believe this? *Will* you believe this? Jesus Christ is going to come back. Every single one of us will be seeing Him – it will be *the* climactic universal event. **Preachers** – when did we last preach this? **Student and youth leaders** – how much does this colour our teaching? **Christian** – how much does this realisation touch every twenty-four hours of your life? **Thinking person** – what action will you take this very day, to start gearing your life towards the all-powerful return of Jesus Christ?

A verse to look up, and then learn by heart: Revelation 1:7.

What action will you take this very day, to start gearing your life towards the all-powerful return of Jesus Christ?

106. Pentecost

Suddenly a sound like the blowing of a violent wind came from heaven and filled the whole house *(Acts 2:2).*

Yes, Christianity is more than a fading memory scrapbook. The day of Pentecost came, to make Jesus accessible, even to the newest follower!

The mystery of Pentecost. The coming of Christ's Spirit reminded people of a wind (unseen, yet powerful in its effects) – and of prophecies such as Ezekiel 37:9. Christians have always loved these vivid descriptions of the Holy Spirit – *wind, fire, oil, water, a dove.*

The sovereignty of Pentecost. 'The wind blows where it wills' said Jesus to Nicodemus (John 3:8). So was the Spirit's working in Acts 2: suddenly there were new believers swept into the Church of Jesus Christ – from lands all around the Mediterranean basin. Don't say the Gospel can't work in certain places and people. It has! It *does.*

The energy of Pentecost. At the start of Acts 2, there were about 120 believers in the church. By the end of the day they had ballooned by over 2,000 percent. And today? Why, to take the statistics of Africa alone, for every little African baby being born today, there will be two Africans becoming followers of Jesus. Pentecost is a phenomenon worldwide!

Pentecost is a phenomenon worldwide!

107. A higher Name

You ... put him to death ... but God raised him *(Acts 2:23, 34).*

Peter's was a sermon to make your hair stand on end. After all, if you, as one of the listeners, had managed to kill the man you hated, it would be a shock to hear that he was alive, and had now turned Judge – on *you.*

1. There's a higher court. The verdict of the religious leaders and the Roman authorities had been decisively reversed! God's verdict overrules that of any human authority, national or international. Appeal, in your prayers this week, *to the top.*

2. There's a higher power. *Death always has the last word.* This was a law of life! Suddenly, over a dramatic week-end, the face of the universe was altered for ever. A man had overcome the grave, permanently. He was not an ex-man – He's still a man ... and if death finds us 'in Him' by faith, we too will live for ever!

3. There's a higher Name. The powerful names of that first century – Jupiter, Zeus, Osiris, Mithras and Diana – were all to be swept off the map through the preaching of Jesus. And today, in our shaking world, men and women everywhere do well to turn to that highest name of all. There is none higher.

> **Men and women everywhere do well
> to turn to that highest name of all.**

108. Salvation in Jesus

Neither is there salvation in any other, for there is none other name under heaven, given among men, by which we must be saved *(Acts 4:12 KJV).*

In 50 years' time grandfathers might be reminiscing, *I saw John McEnroe* … or *Pele.* But here the apostle Peter is preaching the name that spans our whole civilisation.

1. There's power in the name of Jesus. The book of Acts tells of the indomitable disciples of Jesus. Ordered not to speak in His name, they pray. Instead of asking for protection they pray for extra boldness; for more of the same! (Acts 4:29). Here was an unstoppable force. And so:

2. There's prayer in the name of Jesus. We are assured of a hearing when we pray in this name. By His saving death He has won for His disciples a hearing every time we pray. His is the **only** name that *counts* at the supreme court of heaven's throne.

3. There's life and safety in the name of Jesus. Sometimes in international politics, people will speak of 'The Big Three' or perhaps 'The Big Four'. But is there, say, a 'Big Four' of *religion*, big enough between them to establish a gateway to forgiveness and eternal life? '*No!*' said these preachers. *'There's not even two. There's only one!'*

There is only one name!

109. Encouragement

Joseph....whom the apostles called Barnabas (which means Son of Encouragement).... *(Acts 4: 36, 37).*

Here is one of the key figures in the growth of the early Christian Church. And they nick-named him 'Mr Encourager'. How so?

1. His encouragement of a new Christian convert – none other than Paul. Everyone was scared of this former persecutor – but Barnabas mentored him (Acts 9:26-31). And the church grew....

2. His encouragement of a new expansion. Gentiles were pouring into the church – how alarming! But Barnabas was sent. Result: the new converts were affirmed (Acts 11: 22, 23). And the church grew more....

3. His encouragement in the face of new problems. Should new Gentile believers undergo the traditional Jewish initiation procedures? Barnabas was sent, with Peter, to sort it out. 'No', came the answer (Acts 15). It was a vital crossroads. Result: the church went on growing....

4. His encouragement of a new leader for the church (Acts 15:36-40). There was disagreement over whether to drop John Mark for a mission; he was a past failure. *But Barnabas took him on.* Result: Mark ends up 'useful' to Paul (2 Timothy 4:11; Philemon 24). And Mark eventually writes one of our four Gospels!

Do you inspire your fellow-believers? Or do you exhaust them? Be an encourager – and watch the church grow!

Be an encourager – and watch the church grow!

110. Deceit

The feet of the men who buried your husband are at the door, and they will carry you out also *(Acts 5:9).*

Terrifying. Could you withstand a rigorous investigation? The deceit by Annanias and Sapphira couldn't survive in the white-hot purity of the apostolic church!

It wasn't that owning property was forbidden; all giving was voluntary (v. 4). Their sin lay in *pretending* they had given a certain amount, while keeping back part for themselves. 'You have not lied to men, but to God' (v. 4).

The **ironical** element – it's the first flaw in a beautiful story! *'These Christians are no different; they're doing grubby deals on the side just everybody else.'* There's also the **ethical** side. The issue seemed to be, either Christ's *Spirit* must leave the church when deceit set in, or *Ananias* must leave! There was no room for both.

Then there was the **ecclesiastical** factor – this sin dented the whole *church*. Never say that your sin is 'private'. Lastly there was the **eschatological** element – a stern reminder to all, of *future* judgement to come. The lesson is, exercise self-judgement *now*, before the time! Ananias could have repented. If he had, he could have become a leader. He might have been a Paul, instead of being dead!

If he had repented, he could have been a leader.

111. It only takes a spark

You always resist the Holy Spirit! Was there ever a prophet your fathers did not persecute? *(Acts 7:51, 52).*

This sounds like one of the twelve Apostles preaching, or even Jesus. Actually it was Stephen, a man who had been selected originally to serve as an administrator (Acts 6:2-5). But you don't have to be the church pastor, or an Archbishop, or Billy Graham to be an effective evangelist. You can be a tinker like John Bunyan, or a playwright like Hannah Moore.

It only took one person to light the fuse. Stephen's preaching led to his being charged with attacking the Jewish temple – but he meets this challenge by pointing out that *God's activity has never been limited to a building*. He illustrates this from the time of Abraham, the Patriarchs, Moses, David and Solomon. The administrator then turns the tables on his accusers with his punch-line of verse 53: they, the receivers of God's law had never obeyed it. For this bold statement, Stephen paid with his life.

Have you ever heard of one person excommunicating an entire society? This was the sermon that did it. It forced the lock that had, until then, kept the Christian faith confined within its Jewish boundaries and opened it up to the world for ever. Don't say administrators are uninfluential!

It only took one person to light the fuse.

112. God uses all sorts!

The Spirit told Philip, 'Go to that chariot and stay near it' *(Acts 8:29).*

Here's Philip – one of six, appointed to be administrators in the early church (Acts 6:2-5), that is, until – like Stephen – he started preaching!

1. When administrators became evangelists
Powerful, eh? Stephen's sermon (Acts 7) ensured that the church would go international. And Philip's preaching (Acts 8:5-8) caused a revival! But here he is now, witnessing to *one man.*

2. When coincidences become appointments
Philip must have thought, as he set out, *I wonder who I'll meet today. Help me Lord to open my mouth to....someone!* Have you ever prayed like that? And then – by chance, it seemed – there was this Ethiopian official travelling the same road. Something inside Philip said, '*This is it*...run and catch him up!'

3. When conversions become strategies
Here is a non-Hebrew, reading from the Bible book of Isaiah, as he returns to Ethiopia from Jerusalem. A seeker after truth....He invites Philip, 'Sit with me in the chariot, and explain this Scripture to me!' And Philip leads him to faith in Jesus.

Is that how the message of Christ first came to Ethiopia – and thus into Africa? You never know what your witnessing may lead to!

You never know what *your* witnessing may lead to!

113. Saul's conversion

This man is my chosen instrument to carry my name before the Gentiles and their kings and before the people of Israel *(Acts 9:15).*

'The conversion of a great sinner is the best medicine for a sick church', declared the great Baptist preacher C.H. Spurgeon. The persecutor of the church, Saul of Tarsus, was on his way to arrest yet more of Christ's followers, when he was stopped in his tracks on the Damascus Road. *The arrester had himself been arrested.*

Here, in Acts 9, is Luke's account of perhaps the most influential conversion to Christ in all history. With a foothold in three cultures – Roman, Greek and Jewish – history has come to recognise the re-named Paul of Tarsus as one of the definitive founders of modern civilisation.

How he was opposed by the religious and cultural interests of his time! And how he is hated today, by detractors inside and outside the church! They claim that Paul has mangled the 'simple' message of Jesus. But thoughtful readers of the Bible will only endorse Paul's defence in Acts 26:22, 23: **'I am saying nothing beyond what the prophets and Moses said would happen – that the Christ would suffer and, as the first to rise from the dead, would proclaim light to his own people and to the Gentiles.'**

Arm yourself and memorise this sentence.

114. The secret of winning

On the Sabbath we went outside the city gate to the river, where we expected to find a place of prayer. We sat down and began to speak to the women who had gathered there *(Acts 16:13).*

Rod Laver of Australia, widely hailed as the greatest of all tennis players, tended towards understatement. Asked for the secret of winning, he only replied, 'Keep the ball in play, and give the loose ones a bit of a nudge'.

Here's Luke – such a master of the understatement, that you can easily miss the importance of a chapter that glows with New Testament power!

1. Here is the Christian church in its unobtrusive greatness
That riverside at Philippi gave the Gospel its first toe-hold in all Europe – and *there's so little to report!* A few converts, and one housegroup.

2. Here is the Christian church in its unobserved growth
It's God's style to work in simple, unseen ways. As Jesus said, 'The kingdom of God is not coming with signs to be observed' (Luke 17:20).

3. Here is the Christian church in its unheralded conquest
Here is an event of utter simplicity – but all of Europe was to be changed. There would be fierce opposition, but Paul is content to start simply – *and just give the loose ones a bit of a nudge.*

Paul is content to start simply.

115. A life well spent

However, I consider my life worth nothing to me, if only I may finish the race and complete the task the Lord Jesus has given me – the task of testifying to the gospel of God's grace *(Acts 20:24)*.

It began slowly. The mission to Europe began with a single convert, Lydia (Acts 16:14, 15). Paul's 'life' was given, tirelessly, for Christ's service:

1. Working the Empire
Paul trades on his Roman citizenship: on the 58,000 miles of trunk roads that networked the empire, on the *pax Romana*, the peace that prevailed through Roman domination and that gave the Gospel its access.

2. Warning the Nation
Paul never avoided his duty to his own people: by proclaiming that Jesus, once crucified and now resurrected, was their long-awaited Messiah.

3. Waking the Gentiles
It's the great epic of the book of Acts: how the gates of heaven are thrillingly opened to the Gentiles … Philippi, Thessalonica, Berea, Athens, Corinth, Ephesus and finally Rome!

4. Writing the letters
Paul spends a great deal of time in prison (Acts 24:27). But he uses his time well, writing – and so converting a prison cell into a broadcasting studio for the world.

One 'life' spent for the mission of Jesus Christ.

116. John Wesley

The Lord is my light and my salvation *(Psalm 27:1).*

John Wesley, evangelist, was born on June 17th, 1703. He must be rated one of the greatest men who ever lived, and perhaps the greatest man of the eighteenth century. Certainly he was the most widely travelled man of his age, journeying – mostly on horseback – the equivalent of ten times round the world.

It was only after a fruitless mission in North America that he received the salvation in Christ that he had been working so hard to find. 'I went', he said, "to convert the North American Indian, but oh! Who will convert me?'

It was on May 24th, 1738 that Wesley attended a meeting in London's Aldersgate Street, where – through the message of the book of Romans – the light of Christ came to him. As he put it, 'I felt my heart strangely warmed. I felt I did trust in Christ, Christ alone, for salvation; and an assurance was given me that He had taken away my sins, even mine, and saved me from the law of sin and death.'

Over three hundred years after Wesley's birth, we still benefit from the exertions of the two Wesley brothers: John and his 40,000 sermons; Charles and his 7,000 hymns! The two brothers had resolved together, *We are going to change the course of history'....*and they did.

The two brothers had resolved together, *We are going to change the course of history....*and they did.

117. Daniel

And he shall speak great words against the most High, and shall wear out the saints of the most High *(Daniel 7:25 KJV).*

Daniel 7 presents us with a **world-view** with God as the centre; a **world-history**, with Christ as the goal; a **world-stage**, with ourselves, *the saints*, as the pace-setters.

Does it describe you – to be among 'the saints of the most High'? Yet are you aware of a malign opposer whose desire it is to *wear out the saints?* It is true of every generation, and is world-wide at this moment. But if we feel the impact of Satanic opposition, we shouldn't be shaken, for Daniel 7:26 tells us that the oppressor will one day be taken away.

Christian, do you sometimes feel worn out? Be encouraged – at least you represent something that is worth attacking, for the Devil never bothers to attack mere rubbish! This realisation will help us stay firmly on course, and not be pressured to jump to other people's agendas.

Nothing diverted Jesus. 'We've been looking for you everywhere!' people would say to Him. But we don't read of Him replying, 'Oh, I'm so sorry; I hadn't realised – I do apologise!'. He was only too aware that He must be about His Father's business. **Learn to out-last the opposition.**

Learn to out-last the opposition.

118. Genuine faith?

Faith comes from hearing the message, and the message is heard through the word of Christ *(Romans 10:17).*

There are different categories of believers found in every church. Some people are **Mis-believers**. They've picked up various bits of Christianity along the way, but it's all a jumble, and they would never be able to make a clear explanation of what they believe. They need straightening out! Some among us are **Make-believers**. They may have joined the church, but they are deluded as to what a real Christian is. They deceive themselves into thinking that they are in a right relationship with God – but it's all make-believe.

Yet others are **Half-believers**. When things are going well, you will see them in church, maybe at the prayer gathering too. But when the going is rough, and the newspaper headlines are terrible, or when the heat turns on them for their beliefs, they wilt, and opt out of the fellowship. And, we even find **Fake-believers** in the church. They are there for what they can get out of it, money, a position of power, or maybe some flirtation with gullible young people of the opposite sex. Their faith is only a con.

The test is, What exposure are you getting to the word of Christ? Daily, on Sunday and mid-week too? It's only a matter of time, if this genuinely happens, our faith will be proved true and genuine.

What exposure are you getting to the word of Christ?

119. Prayer lists

...you help us by your prayers. Then many will give thanks on our behalf for the gracious favour granted us in answer to the prayers of many *(2 Corinthians 1:11).*

A grand old evangelical minister – Canon Llewellyn Roberts – told of how, during the month, incoming missionary magazines and prayer bulletins would pile up on his desk. News items, financial appeals and prayer requests by the score. Eventually, when the mound had grown too high, he would take them to the rubbish bin, and as he tipped them in, would murmur, *God bless 'em all.* A 'blanket' prayer to cover the world!

Yet *Uncle Llew*, as he was called, was a man of deep prayer. The point he made was that he could not pray for *everybody*; it's vital to be selective. How grateful was the apostle Paul that, in the testing demands on his leadership, he could personally rely on the supportive prayers of 'many'.

Here then is yet another assurance from the Scriptures that **God answers prayer**. It is his chosen way by which we may co-operate with his will. We pray; he works! All the more reason why we should make our prayers specific. We cannot pray for everyone, but we can pray for *someone*. Do you have a prayer list? Why not start one today?

Why not start a prayer list today?

120. Willing to learn?

'My father scourged you with whips; I will scourge you with scorpions.'
So the king did not listen to the people ... *(1 Kings 12: 14, 15).*

This is how the Jewish nation became split into the two kingdoms of Israel and Judah – because their leader decided he knew it all. The spectacular reign of King Solomon was over, and Rehoboam his son had taken over. The elders in Israel's assembly pleaded with the new king.

'It was heavy going, serving your father. Could you ease the burden on us all? Then we'll serve you gladly.' The advice was ignored. 'The whips are going to become scorpions!' was Rehoboam's retort, urged on by his young cronies. *Result* – Israel divided into two warring factions.

If leaders aren't willing to learn, and humbly take advice, one thing is certain. They will have fulfilled the total capacity of their effectiveness by a very early stage. Because they think they have no more to learn, they cease to grow. Many have been the leaders – displaying considerable potential – who nevertheless *have reached their ceiling by the time they are 25*. They never go any further, and it is terrible to see.

The way to keep progressing in the service of God – even when we may reach 90 and more – is to keep hungry, keep humble and keep listening, and stay in the learners' lane!

Keep hungry, keep humble and keep listening,
and stay in the learners' lane!

121. Servanthood

For even the Son of Man did not come to be served, but to serve, and to give his life as a ransom for many *(Mark 10:45).*

The Son of Man was the title by which Jesus most often referred to himself. We have only to read Daniel chapter 7 to understand – from the brilliant, irradiated figure portrayed there – that the name 'Son of Man' (despite its terminology) has undertones of *humanity*, but overtones of *divinity!* No wonder that, at his trial, when Jesus referred to Himself as 'Son of Man' and then quoted from Daniel 7, the charge of blasphemy was made against Him for claiming kinship with God.

Yet the chosen and intended role of this same majestic person was to be the servant of all, during His earthly life. It was service to the very limits, right up to death itself.

And all Christian leadership is essentially defined by the servanthoood of Jesus Christ – with the Cross at centre point. There is to be no strutting, no posturing – not when *he* is our model.

Christian worker, Christian leader, Christian minister – **you and I can achieve nothing effectively for the church until we have proved our servanthood.** We are to make that our aim from day one of any calling that we are given to fulfil.

> **You and I can achieve nothing effectively for the church until we have proved our servanthood.**

122. A biblical world-view

People who want to get rich fall into temptation and a trap
(1 Timothy 6:9).

I was stopped one day in London's Regent Street by a man representing an organisation set up to make people a great deal of money. I told him, 'I don't really care a button about money.'

'But,' he argued, 'we all find it useful. It can solve a lot of problems.'

'I don't know that it does,' I replied. 'It seems to create as many problems as it solves.'

'What makes you say that?'

'Well,' I continued, 'I think about life and it seems to me that quite definitely money is *not* the most important thing. I've also read the Christian Scriptures where we're told that the love of money is the root of all evil. So while I have a use for money, I try to *protect* myself from its grip.'

As we parted, I thought to myself, *Here's a strange thing; I've been talking to a man whose speciality is money, but I actually think I understand money better than he does.*

Develop a biblical world-view and we will find that we can handle not only wealth-creation, but politics, education, sport, sex – and the whole universe – and make sense of them, in and through Christ.

Develop a biblical world-view.

123. Sexual ethics

And such were some of you *(1 Corinthians 6:11 KJV).*

Here in this passage of 1 Corinthians is set out the pagan life-style: idolaters and fraudsters rub shoulders with robbers, adulterers and homosexual offenders, with the comment, 'Do you not know that the wicked will not inherit the kingdom of God?

The miracle of Christ's power is that people involved in such activities were – according to our passage – 'washed', 'sanctified' and 'justified'! Those first-century Christians were bold enough to take on the pagan morals of an entire continent. 'Chastity', wrote William Barclay, 'was the one completely new virtue which Christianity brought into the world.'

I have often heard it argued by homosexual campaigners that – following the freeing of slaves, and the emancipation of women – the next issue to be dealt with is homosexuality.

But there they are wrong. First-century sexual standards (in which homosexuality was rife) comprised virtually the *first* battle-ground in which Christianity met and challenged paganism head-on. Celsus, the pagan critic, flatly disbelieved the power of Christianity to change anything, but the historian T.R. Glover commented about the Christians, 'They *expected* a response….and people *did* respond; they repented and they lived new lives.' *Such were some of you, the Bible testifies.*

Christianity dealt with the sexual ethic a long time ago. Slavery was going to take a little longer. Are you a living part of that *first* victory?

Christianity dealt with the sexual ethic a long time ago.

124. Just one such church ...

Upon this rock I will build my church, and the gates of hell shall not prevail against it *(Matthew 16:18 KJV)*.

I was visiting a country church in England's Cotswolds. It was delightful. The thousand year-old place was brimming with life, beautifully lit inside, and as clean and polished as a gold watch.

The hymns were singable! There was a children's slot. The Bible passage was beautifully read. The preacher explained, illustrated and applied the story of David's sin with Bathsheba. We all greeted one another.

There was prayer for a four year-old – who had had a heart operation six months earlier – who was now running excitedly about in an nearby aisle; it was a joy to see her, and at the end to bend down for a word with her. Here was no irrelevant mumbo-jumbo ritual. *It was real.*

Just one such church – where Christ is honoured, and His word taught – in every village, town and hamlet in the land ... and that is enough to turn any situation and to defy the gates of hell. O yes, it's *hell* that is under attack from the *church*; not the other way round!

When you think of 'the church', don't visualise the hierarchy – for the power doesn't really lie there. **The local church is where the action is**. And that means your church – wherever!

The local church is where the action is.

125. Calvary

And when they were come to the place called Calvary, there they crucified him *(Luke 23:33 RSV).*

My parents were touring the Holy Land. The sun was baking, and there were stones everywhere. My saintly mum had had enough. She sat down on a piece of rubble. 'Where have we got to now?' she gasped.

'*Calvary,*' came the answer.

That made up for everything. Time stood still, here at the centre of everything for all Christian believers; 'The Place of the Skull', Golgotha. But it has a Greek name too. Calvary.

The tour party moved on, but my mother remained seated for a while before rejoining the group. 'For about three or four minutes', she told us later, '*I had Calvary to myself.*'

In fact, you don't have to go to the Holy Land to experience the place where Jesus died for you. He is described as 'the Lamb that was slain from the foundation of the world' (Revelation 13:8). The power of Calvary reaches out to touch people in teeming cities, in icy wastes, in tropical forests. Wherever we are, as we turn in faith to the man who died to forgive us our sins and is now alive as universal Saviour, you can have Calvary to yourself. And time will stand still.

You can have Calvary to yourself. And time will stand still.

126. Does our love show?

Though you have not seen him, you love him *(1 Peter 1:8).*

An up-and-coming artist brought a picture that he had painted, to the great French artist of the nineteenth century, Gustave Dore. It was a painting of Jesus Christ, and he was looking for affirmation.

Dore looked consideringly at the painting for a while and then gave his verdict. *'You don't love him, or you would paint him better.'*

Not that it's necessarily a wise thing to attempt a painting of Jesus Christ at all. The real lesson is that whenever people attempt to portray *anything* of Christ, whether in the arts, in writing, or public speaking – their relationship to him will become apparent. It can't be hidden.

We who have come to believe in Jesus sometimes hear very able performers singing a piece of sacred music. They may not know it themselves, but their very performance is a dead give-away as to whether they love Christ, regardless of whether they get the notes right. It's the same with the public reading of Scripture, indeed with our conversation.

We have never seen him; and yet millions of us love him, and in doing so 'are filled with an inexpressible and glorious joy' (1 Peter 1:8). **If the joy and love are there, they will show in one way or another.**

**If the joy and love are there, they
will show in one way or another.**

127. God's chosen people

Remember that at that time you were separate from Christ, excluded from citizenship in Israel and foreigners to the covenants of the promise, without hope and without God in the world *(Ephesians 2:12).*

Ever been let in without a ticket? It is amazing to Gentile people like myself that somehow we have been let in by the side gate, as far as having a relationship with God is concerned.

We were definitely *not* God's chosen people; we were the outsiders. Then something happened, through a man – himself Jewish-born – who represented Israel and the ancient Covenant to us, fulfilled all its requirements in Himself, and then opened the gate to all who would believe in Him.

How we love the Jews! Why, they form the framework and the fabric of the very cradle that gave us birth, *and we are never to forget it.* But are we required, as they were, to go through the necessary initiations, ablutions and sacrifices in order to participate in the Covenant with God? No – and even the penalty for failure has been endured in a once-for-all sacrificial offering for sins, by this one man, on behalf of everybody, Gentile and Jewish believers together, in a single new entity!

> **For he himself is our peace, who has made
> the two one and has destroyed the barrier, the
> dividing wall of hostility (Ephesians 2:14).**

128. The writing is on the wall

In the same hour came forth fingers of a man's hand, and wrote over against the candlestick upon the plaster of the wall *(Daniel 5:5 KJV).*

The writing on the wall – we use the phrase today to describe the first hint of approaching retribution. Belshazzar's drunken feast, and all of Daniel chapter 5, speak to God's people world-wide of the inevitable fall of wrongdoers.

There on the wall for all the revellers to see were the alarming words that spelt out the coming end of a dictator and of an evil regime:

Mene, mene, tekel upharsin

It was left to Daniel, the faithful servant of God to interpret the message. Literally the words mean *Numbered, numbered, weighed and breakings.* 'Got it, Belshazzar? Your days are numbered, the game is ending; in God's scales you are judged to be a failure; **you and your gang are about to be broken up and replaced.**'

It's God, always God, who has the last word. Anyone out there still staggering from the memory of 9/ll? Any citizens reeling under a totalitarian government? From the bomb-makers of fanatical belief-systems? Any servants of Jesus Christ experiencing religious persecution? The Belshazzars of history have always looked set to stay for ever. But no. Their every action brings closer the day of reckoning. Don't lose heart! The writing is already on the wall.

Don't lose heart! The writing is already on the wall.

129. The depth of the Gospel

Oh, the depth of the riches of the wisdom and knowledge of God!
(Romans 11:33)

You can engage and wrestle with the letter to the Romans, and you will never get to the bottom of it! The same can be said of John's Gospel. The lesson for us preachers and for Bible teachers and youth leaders is huge. Let's state it in a one-sentence principle:

The deeper you go, the wider you will reach

Today there are plenty of people who think the opposite. Faced by an unbelieving age they tend to cave in to the prevailing culture. They hope that by scaling the claims and challenge of Christ down to a bland reductionist minimum they can, in this way, appeal to a wider clientele.

But that is the way of death. *Nothing will ever be heard of their efforts again.* We owe it to the Gospel writers, to the apostles Paul, Peter and the rest, to the blazing witness of the early martyrs, to the uncompromising stance of Athanasius, Tyndale and other mighty thinkers, that the truth of Jesus has reached every continent. Those are the people whose work has lasted. They held to the Gospel message in all its depth, and left nothing out. Try it yourself – and you will reach more people than ever!

They held to the Gospel message in all its depth, and left nothing out. Try it yourself!

130. Inclusive fellowship

Here there is no Greek or Jew, circumcised or uncirmcumcised, barbarian, Scythian, slave or free, but Christ is all, and in all *(Colossians 3:11).*

What a collection they were in that first century bunch of believers! Every type could be found there; yet once they had repented of their sins and come under the banner of Christ's forgiveness at the Cross, the life-styles, nationalities and class distinctions that had marked these people out before, faded into the background; they were now members of a great family of believers.

Sometimes it is said today by untaught leaders, 'Ours should be an *inclusive* church – we ought to open our doors to every category.'

True? Yes, sure – provided it is understood that when burglars, murderers, paedophiles or adulterers are found within the Christian fellowship, they are there as people whose sins have been forgiven, whose past has been wiped out, and who are now in the battle for purity and a Christ-like life-style. 'Such *were* some of you,' wrote Paul.

I remember meeting a con-man in church. Or at least he *had* been a conman. There he was singing the hymns with everybody else! But the past had been confessed; he'd gone to the police, he'd repented and now he'd given up his old way of living.

Inclusive – of all types? Definitely – once we've repented and believed. Christ came for the lot of us.

Inclusive – once we've repented and believed.

131. Jehu's drive

Come with me and see my zeal for the Lord *(2 Kings 10:16).*

Here are two action-packed chapters of the Bible. Jehu is a highly-impulsive operator with an over-active thyroid gland. His anointing by Elisha in 840 BC reads as though they were to light the blue touch-paper and then *run* (see 2 Kings 9:1-3). There would be blood on the carpet.

1. *Question:* Jehu exhibits massive drive (9:20) – but is it harnassed? There was no dealing with Jehu; you either co-operated or you died! Jezebel was the powerful Queen Mum. Surely nobody gets past *her*. Jehu however is more than a match for her – yet somehow we hesitate to declare him a great man.

2. *Question:* Jehu crushes the opposition (9:33, 34) – but what is he replacing it with? Jezebel is killed – and Jehu goes in to lunch. He eats as he drives, with zest. The children of the wicked Ahab are destroyed along with Amaziah's family and all the Baal-worshippers. *But now what?* Easier to pull down than to build up!

3. *Question:* Jehu's got most people sorted – but has he sorted himself (10:31)? We can all see his 'zeal' – but there's too much of 'my' zeal, 'my' side (9:32). Elijah had known weakness; Jehu knew only strength. Elijah prayed; Jehu *drove*. The Bible never speaks of him again.

Maybe history's epitaph for Jehu is … *a magnificent blip.*

**Elijah prayed; Jehu *drove*. The Bible
never speaks of him again.**

132. Jesus the great winner

And there was war in heaven *(Revelation 12:7).*

Shane Warne the Australian cricketer once bowled such a brillliant ball to dismiss England's Mike Gatting, that BBC television featured it in a special sports programme as 'the ball of the century'. I've seen it from every conceivable angle – close-up, behind the stumps, from overhead – and it certainly makes you gasp.

In the last book of the Bible, we read of God's saving act of salvation and victory at the cross of Jesus Christ – *similarly from many different angles*. Here in chapter 12 we are seeing it from the heavenly, the angelic perspective.

The camera is taking us up to see Calvary from the point of view of the angels. *War in heaven.* This is very strengthening to the believer. While the agony of the blood, the nails, the heat and the jeering was taking place below, outside Jerusalem that momentous week-end, the spiritual battle was being fought – and won – in the heavenly realm.

Although Satan will not acknowledge his defeat until the triumphant return of Christ, he is nevertheless a defeated enemy. The fragile saints of God overcome him 'by the blood of the Lamb' (v. 11). **Every time we proclaim the cross, witness and pray, we can insist that evil backs down before Jesus, the great Winner.**

Every time we proclaim the cross, witness and pray, we can insist that evil backs down before Jesus, the great Winner.

133. Sins forgotten

I will forgive their wickedness and will remember their sins no more *(Jeremiah 31:34).*

The worst things we have ever done – and which we would like to forget – have not 'happened' yet in the farther reaches of the universe. Because of the speed at which light travels, something we did ten years ago has yet to take place as far as a distant star is concerned.

What then of the Creator who inhabits all space and eternity? Our evil actions aren't over and done with. They stand out *forever* as an affront to His holy rule. Our every shameful act and word will come back to condemn us at the end of the world when the books are opened and the divine judgement is passed on us.

It is at this point that the miracle of complete forgiveness, prophesied by Jeremiah touches every believer. Are you one such? Can you take it in?

Jesus is *'the Lamb that was slain from the creation of the world'* (Revelation 13:8). The cross straddles our whole existence, and so can cover every sin. So much so that the Creator declares to his believing followers that He cannot even *remember* our faults.

'That to me,' said Billy Graham in a sermon, 'is the most amazing thing about the Gospel. God won't even be able to remember my sins!'

God won't even be able to remember my sins!'

134. Bible study

Were not our hearts burning within us while he talked with us on the road and opened the Scriptures to us? *(Luke 24:32).*

What a remarkable thing to come out with, on that first Easter Day, when it has just dawned upon you that the person you have been walking and talking with on the road is none other than the risen Jesus Christ!

Why didn't those two disciples exclaim to each other, 'Fantastic! To think that we've just seen Jesus!' But they didn't. They were saying in effect, 'What a wonderful Bible study we've just been given!'

Inwardly their hearts were glowing. Jesus had 'explained to them what was said in all the Scriptures concerning himself' (Luke 24:27). The result was something even more lasting and wonderful than a fleeting glimpse of the risen Christ. When you have recognised Jesus in the **Scriptures**, and have in this way been led and introduced to Him, the experience stays for ever. Once you recognise that the Scriptures are all about *Him*, you will never tire of the wonder of Bible study!

Have you *got* a Bible? Are you *reading* the Bible? Are you in a small Bible study *group*? There are myriad thousands of such Bible groups worldwide. Once we join one, our hearts, too, will begin to glow.

**Have you *got* a Bible? Are you *reading* the Bible?
Are you in a small Bible study *group*?**

135. Where are the intercessors?

And he saw that there was no man, and wondered that there was no intercessor *(Isaiah 59:16 KJV).*

'They call it *Ndarasha ya Ngai*', said Dad, '"God's Bridge".' I was eight years old, being driven by Dad in the old battered missionary Ford V8 for a day's fishing. And there it was – a totally natural bridge, formed by a combination of wind and water erosion, not far from beautiful Embu, on the lower slopes of Mount Kenya.

'God's Bridge'; why – in Bible terms – that's ultimately Jesus Christ, who by his saving death interceded between doomed humanity and the God of all purity. But in a lesser way God's people, too, are called to act like a bridge, stepping in by their prayers on behalf of our staggering, dying world. Isaiah's day was not unlike our own – when morals were being reversed (vv. 14, 15) and the upright were being punished.

In every generation God's call goes out: **Where are the intercessors?** It's only here and there that we get a hint of who they are – because for the most part prayer is a hidden, secret ministry. But when the final trumpet is sounded, and the dust and smoke from wicked Babylon have cleared, we shall find out that they were the ones who, under God, were carrying the whole show.

In every generation God's call goes out:
Where are the intercessors?

136. Martyrs for Christ

I saw under the altar the souls of those who had been slain because of the word of God and the testimony they had maintained. They called out in a loud voice, 'How long, Sovereign Lord, holy and true, until you judge the inhabitants of the earth and avenge our blood?' *(Revelation 6: 9, 10).*

Here we take in some of the patterns that can be expected by the Church of Jesus Christ throughout history.

The call of the martyrs across the centuries goes out from 'the altar', because the laying down of their lives is a *sacrifice*. But why are they calling out for vengeance, when Stephen, the first Christian martyr, prayed forgiveness for his killers? The answer is that **the killing of believers is an attack on the Lord they represent**. The call for retribution is not for their own sake but for His. And the 'loud voice' of their call indicates that this is an issue of worldwide importance.

How long before the killing stops and the judgement falls? Why, they – and we – must wait until the martyr roll is finally and eternally complete. Meanwhile our sisters and brothers who are dying for Jesus every hour are clothed in the whiteness of Christ's purity and are in repose. As for us – our part is to pray – and bravely to step into their shoes.

Our part is to pray – and bravely to step into their shoes.

137. Proclaiming a person

Him we proclaim ... *(Colossians 1:28 KJV).*

Yes, it's more than an idea that is being spread around. It is a person, and a person of history that we are communicating. This would have been a completely new idea to the ancient pagan world, even to the most brilliant minds.

'It would sound odd for a man to say he *loved* a god,' wrote the great Aristotle 23 centuries ago. 'The maker and father of all!' A hundred years earlier Plato exclaimed, 'It is impossible to discover; and, when found, it is impossible to declare him to all men.'

And yet today, by God's grace, it is being done worldwide. The proclamation is not in one direction either. Koreans, Africans, Americans and Brits; Chinese, New Zealanders and Singaporeans.... *The good news of God's saving actions in Jesus Christ is criss-crossing everywhere.*

In many places the Gospel is exploding with life and phenomenal growth; in others we are in a holding situation, as a new paganism raises its head and the old ghosts of the past surface once again. **It has never been anything other than hard work, sometimes carried out in the teeth of bitter opposition and martyrdom.**

Plato would have gasped to see it. Are you part of the action?

Are you part of the action?

138. Jesus at the door

Behold, I stand at the door and knock; if any man hears my voice, and opens the door, I will come in to Him, and sup with him and he with me *(Revelation 3:20).*

Having been brought up in East Africa, there is a word spoken by Kenyans that I have always known from earliest days, spoken from the open doorway of our various homes many, many times! It is the word: ***Hodi.***

You say *Hodi* ('Hoddee') when you are seeking entry to a friend's house. The word is never uttered in a loud, demanding voice. You speak it – just loud enough to be heard – in a tone of shy respect and friendly trust. You are saying, in effect, 'I've come. Would you wish me to enter?'

And the reply is 'Karibu.' Or if I was answering in Kikuyu, I would say, 'Uka!' *Come! Come in!*

It is with that tone of friendly approach that Jesus Christ, very God of very God, once crucified for our sins, and now raised as Lord of the universe, stands at the door of every life. He will never storm the citadel of our souls. He stands – hand on the knocker – waiting for the heart's door to be opened by you. *Hodi*, He says. What shall we say?

What shall we say to Jesus?

139. The God we serve

Choose for yourselves this day whom you will serve *(Joshua 24:15).*

What place holds the strongest memories for you? Your first home, perhaps? For Joshua and the people of Israel, it was *Shechem*. It had been Abraham's first stopping place in Canaan (Genesis 12:6, 7), Jacob had pitched his tent at *Shechem* (Genesis 33:18, 19); Joseph's eventful career had begun right there (Genesis 37:12, 13). It was a patriarchal site.

So Joshua's final speech – **to choose who your God is to be** – was given at *Shechem* (Joshua 24:1). Such challenges need plenty of body:

- **Our choices need theology.** Here, Joshua re-tells the calling of the patriarchs, the rescue from Egypt and the wilderness adventures. *God had done it all.* It is remembrance of his acts that fires our choices.
- **Our choices need a morality.** The people acclaim Joshua's challenge, but he's not satisfied. As they re-affirm their decision Joshua instantly challenges them about their false gods (vv. 21-24).
- **Our choices need a liturgy.** How to drive the point home, and make it stick? Sometimes people go forward to register their spiritual commitment at the end of a mission meeting. Here, they renew the Covenant with a large stone under Abraham's famous oak tree. This is why we meet around symbols, sacraments and services – *just as reminders; as 'a witness' (v. 27) to keep us challenged!*

Choose who your God is to be today.

140. Between the times

The blessed hope – the glorious appearing (Titus 2:13).

Ever been to Crete? I have. With its rocky coastline and wild terrain, it was a testing missionary environment for the apostle Paul's younger worker, Titus ('I left you in Crete' – Titus 1:5). Here Paul is writing about the two comings or *appearings* of Christ, and in between that first and second coming, the way of life that Christians are called to exhibit.

1. The past coming of Christ – in grace (v. 11). That first coming, at Bethlehem, was for the *beginning* of the work of salvation on our behalf.

2. The future coming of Christ – in glory (v. 13). The second coming, at the end of history, will be for the *completion* of the work of our salvation – and I note that Christ is described here as 'our great God and Saviour'. Nowhere else in the New Testament do we read of *God* 'appearing'. The truth is that it is the Son who has made Him known (John 1:18).

3. The present life of Christians – in godliness (v. 12). Yes, there is an ethical expectation in this period between the two 'comings', when we are expected to live and witness in a way that is worthy of Him.

**A fine trilogy to meditate upon –
GRACE, GODLINESS, GLORY!**

141. Pray with expectation

... children of God without fault in a crooked and depraved generation, in which you shine like stars in the universe as you hold out the word of life (Philippians 2:15, 16).

Paul writes this from prison, around the year 61 AD. How he loved those Philippian believers – why, they were his very first Christian converts in the whole of Europe (read Acts 16: 6-40). He preached and prayed, and then *expected* them to change, by the power of God's Word and the working of His Spirit. *God's stars*, shining out into darkest Europe!

From then on, they were to multiply as they took the evangelistic message of Christ out into their society. If we believe that this can happen today, then we must apply ourselves in earnest. Do we have a regular church prayer gathering – at a place and time when nothing else is organised in the church? Just to get behind the church's outreach and mission to the neighbourhood? If not, let us announce the first one forthwith....even if nobody comes the first time. Let's not say, 'Oh, our church is dull; it's got no vision.' *It is up to us to create the vision.*

Shall we take hold of this Mission Statement for Philippi, and make it our own, for the next twelve months? And then imagine it happening? No, let's not imagine it; pray, plan and preach it into being!

Pray, plan and preach it into being!

142. Silence – saints at prayer

When he opened the seventh seal, there was silence in heaven for about half an hour *(Revelation 8:1).*

Someone has once said, 'God is the friend of silence.' Understandable, if we've heard the incessant radio music around townships like Nairobi's Pumwani, the shrieking police sirens of New York or London, the barking of the dogs throughout the night in Kampala. But why is there silence at this point of John's vision in Revelation?

It is a dramatic interlude, closing the visions of the seven seals and preceding the awesome seven trumpets of judgement. But as the Bible scholar F.F. Bruce has pointed out, the silence is also connected with 'the prayers of all the saints', in verse 3. *And 'saints' are simply believers.*

The saints, with their prayers, seem insignificant to the 'real' world of restless radio music and clamorous police cars. **The fact is, however, that heaven listens when the saints pray.** Heaven itself goes silent and in John's vision even the praises of the angels seem to come to a halt.

Indeed, the great cosmic actions of God (v. 5) appear to be held back here – until the saints have prayed! This should encourage believers in the power of prayer *to make fresh resolutions about our prayer life.* God listens and heaven itself can fall silent, when the saints are at prayer!

Heaven listens when the saints pray.

143. God is here

Their appearance and their work was as it were a wheel in the middle of a wheel *(Ezekiel 1:16 KJV)*.

Here was a message of confidence from God for the prophet Ezekiel – isolated with his people in the bitterness of exile in Babylon.

The temple of Jerusalem, so vital to the faith of the Jews, was 500 miles away. Soon it would be destroyed by the unprincipled Babylonians. But the book of Ezekiel carries an encouraging message. It is that God:

> **Speaks to His people**
> **Comes to His people**
> **Satisfies His people**
> **Perseveres with His people**

– and does so, even in the hardest and most discouraging of all environments. So there would be no temple soon? Very well. This opening vision of Ezekiel, with its vivid portrayal of a mobile, fiery chariot-temple – featuring a divine, shining human-like figure above it – was bringing the temple to *them*. The Lord was right there with them!

And who is that glowing personage described in Ezekiel 1:26-28? Why, it can only be the pre-incarnate Second Person of the Trinity. The Church is to take heart, even in the hardest places on earth. **Christ is right there.**

Even in the hardest places on earth – Christ is right there.

144. Lifestyle as witness

Therefore, my brothers, be all the more eager to make your calling and election sure *(2 Peter 1:10).*

Yes, there's something for a believer to *do*, when it comes to checking that we really are part of God's chosen 'elect' people. False teachers blandly claim to be God's own people, but their permissive behaviour contradicts the claim – and is an insult to the Christ of all purity. So there is a place for examining the way we live.

Every claim that our Christianity is genuine must be backed up by our lifestyle. *Faith ... goodness ... knowledge ... self-control ... perseverance ... godliness ... brotherly kindness ... love* (vv. 5-7): every true believer in Christ should be beginning to exhibit – or certainly desiring to exhibit – these Christ-like qualities. They do not *make* us Christians; rather they should be the steady, growing *proof* that we have indeed received Christ as Saviour and Lord, and have become Christians.

While we are not required forever to be gazing morbidly into our souls, there is definitely a place for this kind of review, and **making it sure**. And if you, yourself, are uncertain whether you ever really began with Christ, why not go over those vital first steps of repentance and trust in His saving death for you? *It's like writing over in ink what has, perhaps, only been written in pencil so far.* Would you do it now?

Why not go over those vital first steps of repentance and trust in His saving death for you?

145. Vigilance

They watch for your souls as they that must give account *(Hebrews 13:17 KJV).*

Years ago in Kenya, my parents were awoken in the middle of the night by the sound of a violent disturbance from the chicken enclosure near our house. Dad grabbed a torch and went to investigate. Suddenly something slid over his slippered foot. It was a puff adder. A single bite is enough to kill a man. With blows from a stick, the deadly reptile was killed.

But that wasn't enough. The reasoning was, *if there's a puff adder around, there may be a nest somewhere.* It took a little while to find it the next day – but sure enough, there it was, under a log in our garden – with numerous eggs, about to hatch. It had to be destroyed. The hens were saved and so were we children.

Perpetual vigilance. It's a requirement of everyone with responsibility for others. Are you such a person? **Is this your calling on the spiritual front?** In a student or children's group? A house fellowship? A church? For there is danger on every side, materialistic, sectarian, sexual or psychic – liable to strike out at any time.

God's minister and worker is there to protect the family of Christ, through prayer, consistent teaching, and eternal vigilance.

Let us ask the Lord to help us stay on guard.

146. Dead to sin

We died to sin; how can we live in it any longer? *(Romans 6:2).*

Elisabeth and I were seated at a little table on the pavement outside Nairobi's *Thorn Tree* Restaurant. 'We'd love some coffee', we said to our Kenyan waiter. He brought it and said, 'Here's the sugar.' We shook our heads. 'No sugar, thank you.'

The waiter stood stock still in amazement, hands on hips. Bending over us he said, 'So you take no sugar in your coffee! ... WHY?'

Stammeringly I tried to explain that years ago we had taken the decision that we were better off without sugar; that although I did quite like it, it wouldn't make sense to indulge in it now. In a kind of way we had 'died' to sugar.

Later on I thought, *that's what we Christians have done as far as sin is concerned.* Because Christ has died for our sin and its forgiveness, we for our part have declared war on sin and turned our backs on it. 'We died to sin'. Not that we don't face the temptation to indulge in it again, but to do so would be illogical, a denial of all that was meant in our baptism! As with sugar, I must see my sins where they really belong, in the past.

I must see my sins where they really belong – in the past.

147. Love like Jesus

A new command I give you: Love one another. As I have loved you, so you must love one another. By this all men will know that you are my disciples, if you love one another *(John 13:34, 35).*

Yes, it came across as a *new* command, even though such a requirement dated back to Moses' time. Years ago our senior church minister told us junior assistants, 'Over Christmas I've had a vision of a new step forward for our church this year.'

My colleague and I leant forward eagerly. We'd got a bit tired with so much door-to-door visiting. 'A new programme? Wow! What is it?'

'More visiting!'

Here Jesus was calling for more of the same – but with His own new stamp upon the command – and it worked. The historian G.M. Gwatkin, commenting on the quality of Christians' love in the Roman Empire, declared, 'This change from self to unself as the spring of human action is the greatest revolution which the world has seen.'

The real clue to that word *new* is found in Christ's words, **as I have loved you**. No one before had ever loved like Jesus. When people see Christians taking Christ's command seriously, the thought surfaces, *if people love like this, there's only one person that they could possibly be following.*

If people love like this, there's only one person that they could possibly be following.

148. Found as frauds

Woe to them! They have taken the way of Cain; they have rushed for profit into Balaam's error, they have been destroyed in Korah's rebellion *(Jude 11).*

Yes, Balaam is bracketed with two others, noted for the worldliness of their service to God. Balaam is a brilliant oratorical visionary (Numbers 22–24), and yet he is ultimately condemned as negotiating with the heathen king, Balak, and compromising with immorality.

1. Inspiration without character. Balaam's utterances can't be faulted; yet God is not happy about the company he keeps (Numbers 22:9). The apostle Paul in his day had to tell the Corinthian Christians 'You are still worldly' (1 Corinthians 3:1-4). Brilliant preachers, yet ungodly? It's possible!

2. Eloquence without obedience. Here is a very fine speaker and Bible expositor – *yet he is never God's own man.* At one point even a donkey is used by the Lord to rebuke him (Numbers 22: 21-33). And finally:

3. Leadership without integrity. According to Christ, it was Balaam who led Balak astray; he should never have had dealings with him at all. In doing so he gave the heathen king a distorted view of the true God of heaven and a poor example of godly ethics (Revelation 2:14).

Take it in. We can be teaching others faultlessly, and even seeing blessing – and yet be found out at the end of the day as frauds and careerists.

We can be teaching others faultlessly – and yet be found out at the end of the day as frauds and careerists.

149. Living the life

How to live in order to please God *(1 Thessalonians 4:1).*

There are two questions we can ask ourselves daily. *What am I going to learn about the Lord today?* That's theology! And secondly, *How can I please Him today?* That's ethics! The two belong together. **Pleasing God** is what 1 Thessalonians is all about. In this section we see it as:

Pleasing God in your private life – with particular regard to sexual standards (vv. 3-8) –and Paul points out the relationship between ignorance of God and moral laxity. As in Romans 1:18-27, it is so often because people don't know God that they are prone to infidelity, vices and unnatural practices. Spineless ethics come out of poor theology.

Did we ever expect it would be easy? We are following the purest, the holiest teacher ever. If it is *He* who is our model, then we shouldn't be surprised if the way of 'pleasing God' in this respect will be hard, revolutionary, and against the general outlook *of every generation.* Faithfulness **in** marriage (one man-one woman for life: Genesis 2:24), and celibacy **outside** marriage; who's going to buy *that*?!

Answer: those who make it the business of their lives to please God rather than themselves and the existing culture.

What am I going to learn about the Lord today?
How can I please Him today?

150. Captivated by Christ

I consider them rubbish, that I may gain Christ *(Philippians 3:8).*

Until a certain point in his life, the Christian apostle Paul had been obsessed by *religion*. He says so in this very letter, he'd been through the right Jewish rituals, came from the right tribe, was not only 'a Hebrew of the Hebrews', but was one of their Pharisees; why, he could even boast that he was 'faultless' (Philippians 3:4-6).

Then Jesus Christ called him on the now famous 'Damascus Road' and a mighty transformation took place. All else could go! Paul now writes from prison; it didn't matter, for **Christ** had become everything to him.

Years ago All Souls Church was putting on an Easter television programme in church, and the BBC producer, Raymond Short, telephoned the famous Swiss artist, Annie Vallotton, with an invitation to come and draw Easter scenes live, on a screen, as part of the event.

'Are you interested?' he asked. The reply from this Christian woman was memorable.

'I am not interested!' she declared, 'I am *captivated*!' And she came.

This is what happens to all who follow in Paul's footsteps, with regard to Christ. We are not simply *interested* in Christ, as we might be in art or botany. More and more He becomes everything to us. We are captivated.

Are you captivated by Christ?

Subject Index

Christ

1. Begin with Jesus   7
3. The first miracle   9
10. Freedom of the city   16
11. Raise the standard   17
14. Model Christ   20
17. The Bright Morning star   23
25. All is ours in Christ   31
30. Christ our Rock   36
35. Lessons from Leviticus   41
43. Here comes the Christ!   49
46. This man is it!   52
47. Power from on high   53
51. Who is worthy?   57
53. He is here   59
55. A reassuring presence   61
57. Christ's sacrifice   63
62. He comes triumphant   68
68. Christ's ascension   74
74. Resurrection hope   80
93. Everlasting Father   99
95. God sent His Son   101
96. Fear not the future   102
102. Jesus   108
107. A higher Name   113
108. Salvation in Jesus   114
125. Calvary   131
132. Jesus the great Winner   138
137. Proclaiming a Person   143
143. God is here   149
150. Captivated by Christ   156

Ethics

80. Real wealth   86
89. Wars   95
99. Sabbath   105
101. What is man?   107
123. Sexual ethics   129

End Times

36. Wait till harvest   42

48. Look for the signs   54
49. Fear not!   55
50. God is on the throne   56
52. The wrath of the Lamb   58
63. Eternal life?   69
86. Christ's return   92
92. Christ's second coming   98
94. The dragon and the Church   100
103. The sign of Jonah   109
105. Christ will return   111
128. The writing is on the wall   134

Gospel

8. A strange history   14
12. A sense of history   18
13. Still thirsty?   19
16. Come alive!   22
19. Go and wash   25
20. The foolish message of the Cross   26
24. Seize the day   30
27. Spiritual famine   33
29. Who is in control?   35
32. God's great sieve   38
37. Get the centre right   43
39. Saving faith   45
60. Memories   66
61. Spiritual memory loss   67
64. Are you saved?   70
66. Hidden treasure   72
67. Small radical beginnings   73
70. Sons and daughters   76
75. The truth will set you free   81
88. Don't add to Scripture   94
97. The mystery of the Gospel   103
113. Saul's conversion   119
118. Genuine faith?   124
122. A biblical world-view   128
129. The depth of the Gospel   135
133. Sins forgotten   139
138. Jesus at the door   144
139. The God we serve   145
140. Between the times   146
146. Dead to sin   152

Holy Spirit

69. Spirit-filled Christians	75
106. Pentecost	112

Work/Service

2. Leadership and service	8
5. The secret of success	11
7. Meaningless?	13
15. Wake up!	21
18. Are you giving for God?	24
21. Suffering	27
26. Live to give	32
28. Martha or Mary?	34
31. Fool for Christ	37
33. Triumph and disaster	39
34. Persecution	40
40. Do not grumble	46
42. Redeeming the time	48
54. Great days!	60
58. You're more than a number!	64
59. Be different	65
76. Greater things	82
77. Discipleship	83
78. To the ends of the earth	84
79. Giving	85
82. God's touch	88
83. Involved in Christ's mission	89
85. Disciple of Christ	91
87. Called, chosen and faithful	93
90. Who will stand in the gap?	96
91. How do we respond to failure?	97
98. If the Lord is with us…	104
109. Encouragement	115
111. It only takes a spark	117
112. God uses all sorts!	118
120. Willing to learn?	126
121. Servanthood	127
124. Just one such church ...	130
126. Does our love show?	132
136. Martyrs for Christ	142
145. Vigilance	151
147. Love like Jesus	153
148. Found as frauds	154

149. Living the life   155

Characters
4. Enoch   10
23. Rahab   29
38. Noah   44
41. Daniel   47
45. Samuel   51
84. Fanny Crosby   90
100. Job   106
109. Barnabas   115
110. Ananias and Sapphira   116
111. Stephen   117
112. Philip   118
113. Saul's conversion   119
115. Paul   121
116. John Wesley   122
117. Daniel   123
131. Jehu   137

Prayer and fellowship
6. The power of prayer   12
9. Check your Bible   15
22. Pray with expectation   28
56. Where two or three are gathered ...   62
114. The secret of winning   120
119. Prayer lists   125
130. Inclusive fellowship   136
134. Bible study   140
135. Where are the intercessors?   141
141. Pray with expectation   147
142. Silence – saints at prayer   148

Other
44. False prophets   50
65. Remember with gratitude   71
71. Times of challenge   77
72. Revival   78
73. Strength in God   79
81. Pride   87
104. Persecution   110
110. Deceit   116
127. God's chosen people   133